THE 4 INTIMACY STYLES®

THE 4 INTIMACY STYLES ®

The Key to Lasting Physical Intimacy

DR. VIVIANA COLES, DMFT

ISBN: 978-1-7370948-0-7 (Hardcover)
ISBN: 978-1-7370948-1-4 (Paperback)
ISBN: 978-1-7370948-2-1 (E-Pub)

This book is a work of nonfiction. Names and identifying characteristics have been changed to protect their identities.

Disclaimer: The advice and strategies contained herein may not be suitable for every situation. Reading this book does not constitute receiving professional services from any of the parties involved. The author/publisher shall not be liable for damages arising here from. The fact that an organization or website is referred to in this book as a citation or a potential source of further information does not mean that the author/publisher endorses the information that the organization or website may provide or recommendations it may make. Further, readers should be aware that internet websites listed in this work may have changed or disappeared between when this work was written and when it is read.

Front Cover Image by LaJoy Photography.
Cover and Interior Book Design by Wyatt & Co.
Author/Publisher website: www.DoctorViviana.com

Ordering Information: Discounts are available on bulk purchases. For details, visit www.4IntimacyStyles.com.
Printed in South Korea.

TO LOVE!

I THOUGHT YOU'D LIKE TO READ THIS

WITH LOVE

DEDICATION

For my one and only Bobby.

I like you.

I love you.

I choose you.

I want you.

Forever.

Want To

"I want you to ^ have sex."

- DR. VIVIANA

THE 4 INTIMACY STYLES

Contents

THE 4 INTIMACY STYLES

Introduction

I wouldn't be the first to suggest intimacy is important to a healthy sex life, but it can be elusive and seem like an innate quality that couples either have or they don't. The truth is, though we are all born with an inherent capacity for intimacy, different people can have very different motivations to seek or avoid it. My work with clients has revealed the countless ways intimacy can be experienced, as well as the myriad ways partners can differ in their thinking about it and how they prefer to express and receive it. It can seem like a cruel joke, but in my practice, it's become clear that in most relationships there is one partner who needs to feel emotionally intimate in order to be physically intimate, while the other partner needs physical intimacy to feel an emotional connection. The partner who needs emotional intimacy first may only feel safe to engage physically after a series of vulnerable disclosures of thoughts and feelings that are accepted and validated by their partner. For their partner, physical intimacy is actually quite emotional--they feel it's easier to express their feelings through the language of their body. These and other mismatched Intimacy Styles may struggle to intersect in the idyllic space of intimacy, where both partners feel loved and connected. Opposites do attract, but how do opposites *maintain* that attraction?

If both partners' approach to intimacy differs, it can feel impossible to understand each other or to find common ground to integrate their specific needs. It's as if they're taking different routes to meet each other in the same place. Usually, guided by memories of a time when they easily accessed a shared intimacy, they each set out to reclaim the territory of their early relationship, but often cannot find each other there.

I believe that most couples who decide to go their separate ways do so in large part because they've lost the ability to connect sexually. These are couples who can't seem to access the satisfying relational benefits of sexual encounters and over time begin to avoid sexual opportunities with their partner altogether. In severe cases, that avoidance can be so strong that even a simple kiss is dodged so as not to give their partner "the wrong idea." This kind of avoidance can lead to despair and feelings of loneliness as the gulf between them widens. They fear they'll remain stuck in this pattern forever, and either need to accept it or move on. In each devastating case, neither partner envisioned they would end up like this.

The good news is I have found several methods through working with my clients that can counteract, and even prevent sexual disconnect. And after seeing so many couples re-invigorate their sex lives and heal their relationships, I want to share my approach with those who will never get a chance to sit across from me.

Most books about relationships go into great detail about the significance of emotional intimacy. You can expect to find advice about communication, inner child wounds, and how to overcome resentments. While building emotional intimacy is necessary to connect with your partner and feel truly "seen," a key component of achieving it is missing from these books. They tend to stop short at "the good stuff"--*the sex stuff.* And I can say unapologetically that the sex stuff is what this book is all about.

Inside these pages, I will introduce you to my framework for establishing your particular set of sexual needs and wants. I have found that there are four "Intimacy Styles" that determine a person's sexual makeup. Your style will dictate how you experience sex, what motivates you to have sex, and what you need from a sexual partner. You will discover things about yourself you might never have known, and you'll gain insight into your partner's unique Intimacy Style.

Knowing your partner's Intimacy Style will be like finally learning the rules of engagement. It will help you to understand and integrate the conditions and characteristics of their unique style with yours and achieve a bond that deeply satisfies you both. I will also share my experience in helping overcome the unique challenges that accompany each specific style and provide plenty of solution-based strategies for you and your partner to try. There is also a quiz in this book that I urge you to take. It is designed to reveal your individual Intimacy Style, information you can use to more fully understand what intimacy means to you, and communicate what you need from a partner to feel loved and secure.

If you're feeling neglected in the bedroom or pressured; if you're feeling resentful about sex, or worried about how often is "often enough"; if you've ever longed to reconnect with your partner sexually but haven't known where to start--this book is for you. This book can also be a useful guide for couples who already have great sex. Getting to know your and your partner's Intimacy Style will bring your sex life to a whole new level.

I love to help couples achieve their vision of physical intimacy and promote the overall health of their relationship. I love to see the vitality my clients experience--after all, sex is great exercise and a great stress reliever! I'm happy to take this journey with you as you use the methods that have helped so many others. I only ask that you keep an open mind and commit to learning more about your partner. Just like great sex, it will require you to devote some time and energy, but I promise the benefits are worth it and the work will be rewarding. In this book, I will use the terms marriage, long-term relationships, and committed partnerships interchangeably, but these concepts apply to all romantic relationships. Wherever there is intimacy, there are Intimacy Styles. Some case studies in this book are composites of real people and some are fictive. I have changed names and altered any identifying details of clients I have worked with to protect their privacy.

Let's get started on our journey to better, more intimate sex with our partners and claim a new beginning.

INTRODUCTION

THE 4 INTIMACY STYLES

Part I
SEEKING INTIMACY

THE 4 INTIMACY STYLES

Chapter 1
Made For Each Other

Beliefs About Sex

Let me preface by saying: sex is a positive thing. It is perfectly acceptable to have sexual desires and to act on them with another consenting adult. It is not inappropriate, unhealthy, or perverted, to have sex. It is as normal to feel sexual urges as it is to feel nostalgic when you look at old photos or angry when someone cuts you off in traffic--it means you're not a robot.

You may be nodding along and thinking "Obviously, Dr. Viv, we know that--we're not children," but the preface still stands. Not all of us grew up in sex-positive environments; some of us purge the negative beliefs we were raised with, but most will hold remnants of those beliefs in the layers of their consciousness where they can still influence thoughts and behaviors. Not all of us can so easily align what we know to be true with what we were taught to believe.

As a relationship and sex therapist, part of my job is to destigmatize sex for my clients; to give them permission to explore and grow as sexual beings. Another part of my job is to educate my clients and trust me, sex education is needed throughout every age and stage of life. We like to believe sex is intuitive, natural, and spontaneous, just like it is in the movies, without even considering the production crew, the number of takes, soft camera angles, careful editing, perfect lighting, emotionally stirring soundtrack, and *acting* that goes into those scenes. If the reality of a good sex scene requires preparation and work to execute, we should be comfortable accepting a little coaching in our real-life bedrooms.

Sex is indeed natural, but it doesn't always come naturally.

The truth is, we all receive destructive messages about sexuality from society. These messages dictate norms--the approved way to act, when and where to have sex and with whom, how to regard ourselves and our partners, and how it should feel. These messages create a narrative of prescribed male and female behaviors like: "men are always ready to go," and "women don't enjoy sex as much as men do." The damage from either of these examples is considerable. A man who can't immediately or reliably achieve an erection, for example, is completely normal. Almost all adult men have trouble getting or keeping an erection on occasion. But if he's internalized the narrative, he may resist sex with his partner to avoid feelings of shame. A woman who enjoys sex is also completely normal--even healthy! But if she fears that liking sex is intimidating, she may be quite good at denying herself...so good in fact, that she can't even feel aroused by her partner.

Looking through your own history, think for a moment about times and places you may have gotten these kinds of messages, or who they came from. Maybe the message was more general, influenced by the media, and you pieced it together over time. Or maybe you have sharper memories of direct instruction from your parents, teachers, or clergy. Maybe during puberty, when you were eager for as much "advice" as you could get, you absorbed damaging myths circulating at school. In any case, you probably received these messages when you didn't yet have the cognitive skill to critically examine the information--and our cognitive development continues well into our 20s, long enough to register quite a bit of misinformation. You couldn't base future decisions on observed outcomes; you simply accepted the information into your brain's databanks where it remained and found its way into your behaviors. Kids' brains are indeed like sponges, soaking information and holding it there until you come along as an adult and intentionally wring it out.

If you were raised to feel guilty for having sexual urges (as is often the case), it's time to be the adult you needed as a kid, and give yourself permission to be fully human. Just as we might discard the belief that needing support from others is a sign of weakness, we need to unload the toxic shame associated with sexual desire. The shame was never yours to begin with, it was imposed on you by incomplete and imperfect people who struggled with their own limiting beliefs about sex.

You will not die without sex. But I believe sex is essential to our very being, and essential to our relationships with a romantic partner. Sex makes us physically and mentally healthier. Studies have shown it lowers our blood pressure, boosts our immunity, lowers heart attack risk, promotes prostate health in men, and lessens the incidence of incontinence and pelvic floor dysfunction in women. It burns calories, strengthens muscle tone, increases fertility, and decreases sexual dysfunction. It can provide relief from migraines, give us more energy, increase our lifespan, and reduce our risk for stroke. Some studies show it improves memory function, increases mental health satisfaction, and even enhances emotional regulation during conflict, making us feel less distressed and rely less on unhealthy defense mechanisms. I can't think of any drug on the market that can do all of that. In light of this evidence, we should all want our children to grow up to have healthy beliefs about sex, and satisfying sex lives.

——— *Think about it:* ———

Which harmful/helpful messages did you
receive about sex growing up?

Intimacy and Attachment

You can have a satisfying sex life outside of a relationship, but it's no surprise that a foundation of intimacy within a relationship sets the stage for a mind-blowing sex life. Intimacy acts as the glue in relationships. It preserves a bond with our partner because intimacy is the byproduct of attachment-- without it, we don't have as much motivation to seek each other out. When we fail to form an attachment to a sex partner, they lose their allure over time, and their little annoying habits--which we'd be blind to if we developed an attachment to them--seem glaring to us. In the show *Seinfeld*, Jerry is the perfect example of someone seemingly unable to form an attachment to the women he dates. He breaks up with partner after partner during the series' run over the slightest offenses, like eating peas one at a time, or liking a commercial he despises. His sexual desire for them seems to hang by a thread.

In Shel Silverstein's classic children's book The Missing Piece, we're introduced to a small wedge-shaped triangle ("the missing piece") that longs to fit into another shape. Some shapes come by, but none are quite right. Some have too many pieces missing, and others have a missing piece in the wrong shape. A circle with a wedge cut-out rolls by and the missing piece decides this is perfect because not only will they fit, they can also roll together. Only, the missing piece grows. The circle stays the same size meanwhile and says, "I didn't know you were going to grow," and leaves. Eventually a full circle without a cut-out appears and the missing piece says, "I think you are the one I've been waiting for. Maybe I am your missing piece." "But I am not missing a piece," says the full circle in response. The missing piece expresses disappointment because they were hoping the two of them could roll together. The full circle explains that they will see they can roll by themselves if they try, and the more they do it, the more their edges will soften and round. The missing piece hurls itself up and over and with more repeated attempts, softens so much it turns into a full circle itself. The story ends with a picture of the missing piece, now a full circle, rolling alongside the other full circle.

Attachment and intimacy work in much the same way. We tend to long for a person with whom we can merge, and try to wedge ourselves into various partners' corresponding gaps to feel complete. Often we find that we fit for a while, then outgrow the relationship. In the extreme, this looks like Jerry quickly losing interest in a partner for some obscure difference and breaking away to find another shape to try on, hoping to be made whole. Yet wholeness can never be achieved through another. It's as if humans were blueprinted in the womb and long to be "one" with a person they're symbiotically dependent on. Unfortunately, that option was severed with the umbilical cord. We're meant to be distinct entities whose relationships are not parasitic, but chosen.

You see, we need not for our partner to be identical to us or an extension of ourselves, but to be a safe base for us to launch ourselves into the world and then return, again and again. Like all of us, Jerry needs a person who respects and encourages his freedom and wholeness while also being safe enough for him to be vulnerable and rely on them to meet some of his emotional needs. It's within this balance that intimacy thrives, particularly sexual intimacy. We don't complete each other in the act of sex, we "roll together" enjoying the dimension both partners bring to it. Sex becomes itself a kind of safe base to which partners can return and gain strength and stability to power them through the lives they lead, both separately and together.

> *To be chosen, again and again, checks the box for one of the greatest human needs: to be desired.*

Intimacy is at work here too, as the formation of intimacy requires confidence in each other, and the confidence that your partner desires you will allow you to express equal desire for them.

The Evolution of Intimacy

We evolved to be in frequent contact with fellow human beings in communities and families, and data from many studies suggest that we are profoundly influenced by our social bonds. We evolved to form attachments to others as a survival strategy, so if death are the stakes, it's no wonder we feel we need someone to "complete" us. If our primitive ancestors could effectively cooperate to find food and shelter, and if they were bonded enough to others to risk their own lives for them, preservation as a group was more likely. Even now, as technology and globalization make an independent life doable, we suffer without others. We have a powerful motivation to seek connection, as a lack of attachment to friends or partners is associated with a variety of consequences to our physical and mental health.

According to *Scientific American*, our brain's default mode, the state it returns to when it's not actively engaged in goal-oriented tasks, is mainly concerned with others. In this state we daydream, our thoughts centering on ourselves in relationship with others. It is as if our self-concept cannot stand alone and only exists against the backdrop of others. We reflect on our social connections more than we realize, constantly sizing ourselves up in comparison to others and considering how we fit into dynamics with coworkers, friends, family, etc. We use input from others to inform our view of the world and how we should think, dress, and conduct ourselves. Culture would likely be impossible to cultivate if no one cared what other people thought. We would not organize our behaviors around the principles of our era, and every group-dependent phenomena, from government to fashion trends, wouldn't exist. It's clear that the genetic predisposition to identify with others was selected and passed on by our ancestors for a reason.

Acceptance from others is fundamental to our ability to thrive, and the relationship we have with our primary partner gives us our greatest sense of belonging. This primary bond acts as a reinforcement from outside threats, shoring up our resilience. If this relationship is healthy, we find within it a safe space to grow, to seek and receive comfort and support, and a sense of definition and purpose. These relationships are some of our most valuable and precious investments, and learning healthy sexual intimacy is one of the greatest ways we can protect that investment. It doesn't matter if you believe emotional intimacy is more important than sexual intimacy. What I hope this book gets across is that the two are interconnected and you can't have one without the other.

In Your Best Interest

Being in a committed relationship is also a great way to live. It's become common knowledge that, on average, married men and women enjoy healthier, longer lives and build more wealth than their single counterparts. We now know just being in a long-term committed relationship confers similar health benefits and increases life satisfaction. Both marriage and cohabitation have been shown to lower levels of the stress hormone cortisol, replacing it with oxytocin, "the love hormone," which is released when interacting, cuddling, or having sex with a partner.

In a landmark study, married women were hooked up to brain imaging (fMRI) scans and told they were going to receive a small electric shock. As expected, activity in their hypothalamus, a brain region associated with stress response, increased. If no one held their hand or if a stranger did, these levels of arousal did not dissipate. But their stress response decreased markedly when their husbands held their hand. Further, the higher the women rated their level of marital satisfaction, the more their brains calmed down--some of these women even returned to baseline. This is a powerful testament to the benefits of companionship and the importance of a committed relationship to our evolution. Just the proximity of our partners and the feel of their touch can literally decrease the amount of cortisol in our bloodstream and the chemicals in our brain that alert our nervous system to the presence of a threat. The greater our bond and the more contact we have, the greater our ability to not only withstand stressful events, but completely overcome them.

With perks like these, we should all rush to be partnered, or if we're already partnered, we should do our best to ensure a high level of satisfaction in our relationships. And yet, the benefits of intimacy seem so far out of reach for so many. If we evolved to form attachments as a strategy for self-preservation, and if our brains are so often concerned with gaining acceptance and belonging from others, why is it so hard to create and maintain intimacy? Well, like most things in life that are worth it, intimacy isn't easy. The rewards don't come without risk.

THE 4 INTIMACY STYLES

Chapter 2
The Illusion of Permanence

The Long Term

You've heard about the top three "marriage killers": money, sex, and kids. It might surprise you to learn that in my experience working with couples, there's only one true assassin: sex. It may not be cited as the cause for the breakup, and these couples may not consciously accept that sexual disconnect played a part, but left unattended, dissolving intimacy will leak into and corrode every aspect of a relationship. It rarely gets the attention and treatment it deserves, but the negative impact of this issue cannot be underestimated. Without healthy physical intimacy, relationship satisfaction simply cannot be maintained. Since 2003, I've worked with thousands of individuals who are unhappy in their relationships. They typically come to me with despair in their eyes and desperation in their voices. With bodies slumped, they describe going from "Can't Keep My Hands to Myself," to "Can't Touch This." Invariably, they recount how their experience of dry spells and ruts have eroded their feelings toward each other, leading to contempt. They often experience daily discord. Without exception, they express bewilderment at the sexless state of their partnerships--none of them set out to have a platonic marriage. On the contrary, most couples have a strong start in the bedroom and assume their natural and spontaneous connection will last. They're aware of the sexless marriage trope, but a heady cocktail of bonding hormones blinds them to the possibility. Over time, "that won't ever be us" turns into "how did this happen?"

In our society, we tend to accept that love will transform over time, but rarely do we acknowledge that shared sexuality will also change. We have no roadmap that explores the often-bumpy terrain of long-term monogamy, nor do we acknowledge how difficult it is to sustain attraction and lust with one partner. We're taught that monogamy is our destiny; a universal milestone and necessary for a happy life. We're expected to choose "the one" in the earlier half of our adult years and hope they're the missing piece that fits us perfectly and remains firmly in place forever. Or, if they do shift around, they do so alongside us in a way that corresponds with our own movement.

We also have no blueprint for experiencing intimacy outside the model of monogamy and there is no culturally accepted space for exploring alternatives. Yet in the search for intimacy we are encouraged to sample as many flavors of potential partners and relationships as possible. These days, dating apps make it easy to practice monogamy in a series of trial runs. Eager to enter into the contract of our fate, we put our dating partners to the test, checking to see if they embody the modern standard, which is a person who delivers the benefits we used to rely on our community to provide: identity, intellectual stimulation, passionate love, deep friendship, help with children, financial support, security, and purpose. If they inevitably disappoint us in any of these categories, we're taught not to question the soundness of monogamy or consider how we might outsource some of these. We simply dedicate ourselves to finding the next person with whom we can trial the benefits of marriage, someone who might finally carry the necessary array of traits to make us feel complete and happy for the rest of our lives. You have to admire the hope in this endeavor, but with each failed relationship and each effort to choose better, the optimism gradually fades, replaced by doubt. Despite our desire for the mythical "one", we start to question how realistic it is to land an ideal partner and consider settling for a "good enough" partner. Yet the 50 percent divorce rate for first marriages and 65 percent for second marriages seem to suggest that "good enough" won't silence our inner directive to find "the best." Monogamy may not be working for us the way it is supposed to but if we get it wrong, the specter of our soulmate inspires us to try again.

Considering the endless wheel of disappointment and renegotiation we enter into with destiny, it's no wonder that over the past 20 years, the rate of delayed marriage (in favor of cohabitation) and the existence of so-called "never-marrieds" has risen dramatically. The social pressure to get this monumental decision right, combined with the existential limitation that comes with refusing all future potential loves (perhaps even "the one" we should've held out for), is more than some young people can bear. A report from the Pew Research Center shows that 1 in 4 of today's young adults are projected to eschew the institution altogether, suggesting that our modern promise of monogamy is suspect. Or at least, we haven't yet figured out how to achieve lifelong happiness with only one flawed person when thousands of potential mates are available, literally at our fingertips.

On top of that, in western culture our streak of individualism causes us to feel we need to find our own solutions to problems, or if we can't, we should at least suffer them behind closed doors. This social practice creates the illusion that other couples are managing just fine and our struggles must be some kind of moral failure. Meanwhile, most of us grew up in communities and families filled with models of unwavering monogamy; couples whose marriages may not have been outwardly romantic but were a study in cohesion and stamina. We might never have contemplated their sex lives or relative happiness because neither seemed relevant. Simply remaining married was the success story, a belief that persists in our cultural narrative as we clamor for the "secret" from couples who have made it to old age intact. It might never occur to us that the couple celebrating their 50th anniversary might also suffer in silence. Discretion does not always equal success...no news is not necessarily good news.

Because we don't see our crisis represented in others, we can't appreciate how common it is to experience waning desire. Even when couples divorce over it, it is rare for them to admit it. Many who do confess they divorced for this reason are shamed for being immature or superficial, or not giving their marriages enough of a try. It seems no amount of misery in the bedroom can justify walking away...partners who have been denied intimacy for 10+ years have been considered defectors because, in the exasperated wisdom of their family and friends, "sex isn't everything." Outsiders will understand any other unmet need as grounds for divorce, but somehow the need to be intimate with one's lifelong partner is hotly debated and often considered superfluous. This response makes it clear that even if we can acknowledge that sex is healthy, we still don't grasp how profound its importance is to relationships. When one partner exempts themselves from sex, they tend to have many reasons and often they feel guilt, but they almost always see their case of sexlessness as a nonnegotiable fact. "This is just how I am," they seem to say. They don't understand that levels of desire are constantly in flux.

The nature of passion is not static and the lack of it is not a permanent condition.

Just as some days you're more in love with your partner than others or some days you don't feel any love for them at all, desire also ebbs and flows.

The One and Only

It's the couples who draw a hard line between their separate intimacy needs and consider them inviolable states of being that need realistic expectations of intimacy over time, as well as help balancing their highs and lows on the desire spectrum. These couples need to understand that rather than a destination, intimacy is more like a highway, with occasional detours and distractions, rest stops, and long stretches that can either be pleasant to ride through or feel flat and uninspiring. And navigating the intimacy highway as a couple is not as intuitive as we're led to believe. Many couples assume that if they are coasting sexually, they are succeeding. What they don't realize is that if they coast for too long, they won't have any built-up momentum to get them over bumps in the road, much less the occasional hill.

HOW DO YOU KNOW IF YOU ARE COASTING SEXUALLY?

- Have your sexual interactions become predictable and boring?
- Have your sexual and sensual experiences become less and less frequent?
- Have you begun to avoid any conversations with your partner about your sex life?

If you answered "Yes" to 2 or more, you may be coasting your way to a big problem.

Let me be clear: I see the benefit, both short and long-term, of nurturing a strong friendship with your partner. Studies have shown that the quality of a couple's friendship correlates to better management of conflict within the relationship. It certainly enhances quality of life to regard your partner as your best friend.

But your sensual bond with each other is the one thing that separates your partnership from any other relationship you have.

When I've asked my clients why they believe sex is an important part of their relationship, they usually say, "Because it's part of any healthy relationship," I nod knowingly and then ask, "But why?" After staring at me blankly, I bail them out and say, "Sex is important because it's the *only* thing you are expected to do with your partner and no one else." I go on to describe that we are allowed to share beds with friends, our doctors see us naked, we even say "I love you" to pets. Sexuality is reserved for our partners. But keeping sex sacred only means something if you are actually having it. You don't get credit for not sharing your sexuality with others if you are not having sex with your partner--the one you chose over everyone else.

The access you have to touch each other's bodies or to gaze into each other's eyes is a privilege. Over time and through joint experience you and your partner co-create a detailed sensorial map of each other. You know each other's favorite places to be touched, moles and birthmarks, turn-ons and turn-offs. You share thoughts, feelings, and fantasy you wouldn't disclose to anyone else. You orient your sexuality within the context of this shared world, a place e.e. cummings described when he wrote "I like my body when it is with your body."

Even in relationships where sexuality between partners is restricted due to physical limitations, there still exists a shared world if only mentally, with its unique and private pleasures. And it is also possible within these restrictions to address one of the most urgent and universal needs in a sexual partnership: feeling desired by one's partner. We need our partner to express their appetite for us and us alone--for them to elevate us above all others.

Many of you are reading this book because you feel like your partner no longer appreciates your unique bond, no longer reveres you above all others, and your exclusive, shared world has downgraded into a casual friendship. Or worse, you feel like you've become roommates whose only interaction is to pass messages before retiring to separate rooms.

The Problem of Priorities

As adults, we do a juggling act, and some of us have so many balls in the air we can't expect to catch them all on the descent. There are some we let go of. There are some we won't allow ourselves to drop. And curiously, there are others that we seem to believe will just hover, suspended in air until we get around to catching them. Our relationships tend to be one of those suspended balls. But, as we all know: what goes up, must come down.

The balls we juggle are benign, humdrum everyday tasks--work, parenting commitments, social obligations, housework. But just as the presumption of certainty kills eroticism, the mundane poses an existential threat to intimacy. Many couples have unintentionally turned toward the routine duties of life and away from each other, letting these constraints absorb their attention, buy up their time, and take priority. While they don't mean to, these couples have gotten into the habit of permitting a never-ending litany of to-dos to deplete their sexual energy.

And while the problem may begin as a one-off dry spell, it can easily become the norm.

If you have young children, it is especially easy to get locked into a burdensome and complex juggling routine that you have no hope of getting right. As a parent, you're expected to do more than you're humanly capable of and many of us try--and end up transforming our partnerships into 24/7 co-parenting units.

Parenting throws continuous challenges our way, one after the other. We scramble to adjust and educate ourselves on each new stage our children enter and just around the time we feel confident, they're onto the next. Because we can't be perfect parents, we must settle for good enough, but we're doing so in the modern era of parenting, which is to say, guiltily. Sometime between our parents' generation and our own, the culture of having and raising kids shifted significantly. It used to be that children existed in a grown up's world--they followed and observed the work and recreation of their parents. If our parents wanted to watch the news for example, we were expected to watch too or go elsewhere. Now our children control what's on tv (ask any parent of young children how many times they've seen *Frozen* and that becomes clear) as well as pretty much everything else that goes on in the home. The centralization of children in the family structure has ousted the parents as heads of the household and produced a narrative that raising children means sacrificing ourselves to endow them with everything we have. These days the message is clear: while the standard of perfect parenting is impossible, we are expected to strive for it anyway.

And so it follows that the energy that should go into sustaining our relationships goes instead to the children. We're pressured to cultivate every experience for our children, much like we used to use our creativity to plan quality time with our partner. We're meant to arrange and oversee every detail of their lives, ever mindful of their needs, which--unlike the care prescribed for children of earlier generations--go far beyond the basic needs of food, shelter, clothing, safety, and love. According to our cultural narrative, modern children need responsibility but also freedom, recreation but also enrichment, sensitivity but also grit, education but also unstructured time, nurturing but also independence. Such an exhaustive and contradictory list requires from parents a tireless zeal; this on top of the basic, but no less demanding caretaking duties. What would life be like if we devoted half of this drive to our partners?

Our parenting culture demands that even the intimacy we have with our partners be diverted to our children.

The way we talk about our children ("I would die for them," "they are my world") is, in a way, romantic. Not romantic in the sense of romance, but in the sense of an idealized love. The earnestness and devotion we feel for our children and present to the world is not dissimilar from the feelings we would express about a love affair ("I can't imagine life without them"). It is expected that we cherish our children and of course we do, but in the present-day model, ardent affection and constant affirmation is puzzlingly better suited to our parenting style than it is our partnerships. In fact, the notion of delighting in our partners with the same level of rapture we devote to our children often strikes us as frivolous. "My partner is a grown up," we seem to say, "they can handle themselves." And so we accompany our children, sometimes lying beside them and rubbing their backs or stroking their hair, as they drift off to sleep. Our eyes light up when we see them after school or daycare. When they're hurt or troubled, we hold them in a long embrace. There is nothing wrong with any of this, and I believe it's healthy that children experience more warmth and affection from their parents than in generations' past, but it seems that our partners deserve some of this romantic and intimate energy. Instead, they often get the leftovers.

In fact, I've had clients who find themselves jealously coveting the attention their partner lavishes on the family dog. After a long day of work, their partner doesn't walk in and greet them with a kiss, or even a hello. But they do enthusiastically reunite with the equally ecstatic dog, inviting the dog into an embrace with outstretched arms and a huge grin on their face. Unfortunately, this is not a unique complaint. If you google "the dog gets more attention than me," you'll get 311,000,000 hits. Among the search results, "15 Signs Your Significant Other Loves A Pet More Than They Love You" comes up, as well as an exasperated husband who speculates in a letter to "Dear Abby" that his wife would rather he sleep on the dog bed, and the dog sleep with her. Dejected partners in this situation may wistfully note that the photo roll on their partner's phone is densely populated with pictures of the dog, but no recent photos of them. Or that if you were to go by their social media, their partner would appear to be in a relationship with the dog, not them. Or that the dog hears frequent affirmations that they're "handsome" or "adorable" while they can't recall the last time their partner paid them a compliment. In order of priority, these partners have been deserted at the very bottom.

─────── *Think about it:* ───────
Which priorities take precedence over your sex life?

The Death of NRE

Let's ponder *why* two people who are in love would ever lose their spark and put each other last. Because all couples experience NRE (New Relationship Energy), the by-product of a powder keg of neurochemicals, it's hard to grasp how two people so intoxicated by each other could come to see their partnership as unstimulating.

The syndrome of fading NRE can be painful to experience and can seem to come out of nowhere, but has its origins in the attitude I just mentioned. It's counterintuitive but having absolute certainty in your relationship and regarding your partner as a stable, permanent fixture can predict an eventual erotic demise. The concept of eros, meaning sensual or passionate love, has another broader definition that corresponds to a source of aliveness. We feel the energy of eros when our minds switch from multitasking to a "flow state" in which productivity and creativity seem effortless. We feel it when we connect with nature or feel connected to others, in the pursuit of our dreams, and in moments of high self-esteem. In contrast, the convention of marriage, with its emphasis on domestic affairs, reduces spouses to business partners. The utility of this arrangement, despite its mutual benefit, threatens to snuff out the flame of erotic energy.

Ponder this: in the beginning, we were powerfully inclined to attract our partner's interest. We presented ourselves as best we could; as sparkling conversationalists, confident, funny, sexy, and worldly. We paid careful attention to the clothing we wore and our body language. We compulsively checked our hair and freshened our breath. We thought about them all the time--they invaded our thoughts to such an extent that we couldn't experience anything without imagining their opinion of it. We obsessively catalogued their preferences, memorized the things they said, and treasured souvenirs we borrowed or they left behind; his t-shirt, her favorite mug. We showed enthusiasm when they spoke about what they loved, listened to the music they listened to, and learned about their favorite hobbies. We watched the movies they wanted to watch, went to the restaurants they wanted to try, read the books they recommended. We happily helped them move or drove them to the airport--anything to enter into our beloved's world and increase the moments of closeness between us. We seduced them, and they enraptured us.

We wanted closeness because we were so aware of our separateness. Love and sexual attraction activate the amygdala, the brain's fear center. The rapid beating of our hearts and flutter in our stomachs came from our insecurity. We knew our partner could easily survive without us; we'd only just met. And before that, as far as they were concerned, we *didn't exist*. Now we were auditioning to be a permanent part of their lives and did our best to get the role. Unfortunately, once we had it, we stopped trying to be worthy of it. It was as if our partner had always been there, and always would be. But what if we could discard the illusion of permanence with our partners? We might see the truth: our partners are *still* capable of surviving without us. I'm envisioning the far-off look in your eyes as you re-read that last sentence. It's true: you would both survive without one another.

What if we dedicated a third of our once-potent New Relationship Energy to our present-day relationship? What if we expressed interest in our partner's aspirations and dreams? What if we tried to impress them? What if we stopped assuming our partner's devotion, and instead of claiming them as "ours," acknowledged they are thrillingly independent of us? It may strike couples as illogical, but if they want to yearn for each other, they must trade comfort for the unknown.

> *We can't crave what is already on our plates...we cannot ache for what we feel entitled to.*

In the same way that sought-after possessions, once owned, are less enticing to us than when we wanted them, our partners are more beguiling to us when we can only anticipate having them. And once we're clear that we cannot actually *have* them, longing will replace our certainty. In the case of marriage, this longing can incite us to chase our partners for a lifetime.

───── *Think about it:* ─────

What would it look like for you to dedicate a third of your once-potent New Relationship Energy to your present-day relationship?

THE ILLUSION OF PERMANENCE

THE 4 INTIMACY STYLES

Part II

PEELING BACK
THE LAYERS OF INTIMACY

THE 4 INTIMACY STYLES

Chapter 3
The Mind-Body Connection

Silence Speaks Louder Than Words

Almost every relationship expert focuses on communication. Books about repairing relationships will inevitably address it, and sometimes the goal of therapy is simply learning how to do so. But even the most reserved couples communicate, and they do it all the time. Eye rolls, crossed arms, a downturned mouth, turning a cheek instead of accepting a kiss, letting out an exasperated sigh. This is lively communication, and for couples in conflict, it's ongoing.

Lack of intimacy often appears to be the sole doing of one individual in a relationship until you consider the silent and barely detectable language of couples. A withering sex life is a hot button in relationships, and couples often won't bend to meet each other in the middle. They're often tempted to blame each other for their lack of chemistry, but whether they realize it or not, both push each other away through non-verbal cues like averted eye contact, stony glares, and awkward silence. They claim they're avoiding the subject altogether, or "picking their battles," but there's an implicit understanding that runs like a current between them and that will someday explode into explicit conflict. In the absence of a verbal discussion neither can deny engaging in, the avoidance that speaks louder than words will poison their relationship and drain them of their emotional intimacy, leaving very little hope for physical intimacy.

John Gottman, a relationship researcher and clinician who claims to be able to predict whether a couple will divorce or not by observing their behaviors, has discovered through clinical study that there is a "magic ratio" of interactions between couples. According to Dr. Gottman, happy couples average a 5:1 ratio during periods of conflict, which means for every negative feeling expressed or negative behavior, there are 5 positive ones. These interactions might be small, barely noticeable moments where one partner makes a bid for attention, say by offering an apology. If the other partner ignores them, rolls their eyes, or worse, lashes out at them accusing them of insincerity, it becomes a negative interaction. If the other partner accepts or simply acknowledges their partner speaking, it becomes positive. In unhappy couples, the ratio of positive to negative registers at 0.8:1, a number that reflects the non-verbal or barely verbal negative interactions that often come to define a couple struggling with physical intimacy.

———— *Think about it:* ————

What are you non-verbally saying
to your partner about sex?

Stress Lives In Our Bodies

Couples who argue with body language need to disengage and physically reset, not just with each other, but within themselves. Our modern culture has many advantages, but it has also invited more stress into our busy minds and bodies. Conflict, trauma, and the pressures of work leave their imprint in the form of muscle tension, aching joints, high blood pressure, sleep problems, imbalanced hormones, gastrointestinal distress, psychiatric disorders, and dependency issues, just to name a few. On top of this, we're an increasingly sedentary culture with less and less opportunity to engage our senses and move our bodies. This compounds an evolutionary safety mechanism built into our nervous system; in response to stress, we can either fight, flee, or *freeze*. When stress becomes pervasive, as it often does in our busy lives, our bodies remain on high alert, responding as if to a major threat, and often that response is to go numb and dissociate, perhaps by doom-scrolling on our phones or escaping into Netflix. In this state we can't connect to our body...so how could we desire physical intimacy?

In the book "The Body Keeps The Score," Dr. Bessel van der Kolk writes

that the natural state of mammals is to be somewhat on guard. However, in order to feel emotionally close to another human being, our defensive system must temporarily shut down. In order to play, mate, and nurture our young, the brain needs to turn off its natural vigilance.

It can be helpful to engage in mindfulness practices that connect us to the breath; it can also help to engage in playful or relaxing physical activity with our partners, like dancing or taking walks together. These somatic exercises will rewire the connection to our physical selves, allowing us to fully inhabit our bodies and experience our sensations. Doing any kind of physical exercise with your partner has also been proven to create positive associations leading to greater relationship satisfaction. In fact, because exercise induces the elevated heart rate and sweaty hands common to early attraction, exercising together can lead partners to experience a renewed romantic interest in each other. Couples will also mirror each other's movements as they exercise, a process called nonverbal mimicry that makes people feel emotionally attuned with one another. This shortcut to emotional bonding can be especially beneficial to your intimate life.

It can also be helpful to employ grounding techniques, in which you use your five senses to notice and feel the tangible world around you might also be helpful. Slow down and listen to what sounds are around you, focus on what you can feel in different parts of your body, eat or drink something and savor its taste, or breathe in an aromatic scent.

Checking in this way with your own body when your partner is near may help you to welcome their touch or inspire you to reach out and touch them.

Predictably, enhanced physical awareness can lead to greater sexual satisfaction which is why a sex therapy technique known as "sensate focus" is often prescribed as a way to reconnect sexually. I believe this approach is valuable, but really only beneficial for couples who feel safe being vulnerable with each other and want to enhance their sex life with the quality of intention. This is why I developed my own version of it for couples in crisis called The Dr. Viviana Method for Intimate Reconnection©, which can be found on my website at DoctorViviana.com. Traditional sensate focus draws awareness to the sensations of touch and being touched through sessions of prolonged physical contact that gradually advance from only sensual touch (ie., no breasts or genitals) to sessions that include sexual parts of the body and eventually a session of intercourse that follows the same guidelines of slow, intentional contact.

In my version, couples engage over 6 weeks' time in a daily practice that includes activities to nurture their emotional intimacy as well as their physical intimacy. They start by simply embracing and sharing brief, scripted affirmations with each other. The script gives partners the words they might otherwise struggle to come up with, and the repetition of these messages as more is added on each day has the same impact as it would if the sentiment was their own. Language is powerful in relationships, and this exercise re-trains partners to speak to each other with respect and love. Each week the couples are asked to schedule time to do specific exercises meant to increase their ability to listen and share with each other to build their emotional bond, and each week another of these exercises is added. Gradually, sessions of physical contact involving brief massage, sensual and sexual activities are added, and the time allotted for these, plus the amount of physical contact allowed are built upon each week. Much like in traditional sensate focus, these earlier sessions of physical intimacy do not contain any goal other than experiencing the sensations of sensual touch. But eventually they advance to be more sexual in nature. I have found that the slower pace and inclusion of relational bonding exercises is a better fit for couples experiencing conflict. It eases these couples into the experience, freeing them from fears related to vulnerability and gives them tools to repair their ability to communicate, both emotionally and physically. This gradual, progressive method ultimately gives couples a committed time and space to absorb the sensations of desire and connect them to the smells, tastes, and textures of their partner's body.

When we can fully inhabit our bodies and feel the sensations it creates or receives, we can be more aware of ourselves, and stop reacting to our partner as if they're a threat. When we can feel discomfort without fear, when we can recognize times we're holding stress in our bodies, and when we can allow our jumbled thoughts to arise without adding our panic to them, we are in a better place to accept our partners without judgement. When we're no longer hypervigilant, scanning our partner's body language for warning signs, we might be able to notice when they're distressed without taking it personally. Offering support in these moments instead of dissociating solidifies trust. It says without words: I see you, I won't disappear on you, and I won't ignore your feelings.

The Unconscious Logic of Denied Intimacy

I've presented the probable causes behind a weakened intimate bond, and how most of these are attributable to the stress of daily life. I've suggested that taking our partner for granted can lead to diminished NRE, and I've discussed how our bodies communicate and take in hostility. And yes, typically these obstacles make up the immediate problem of low intimacy.

But what if every obstacle is removed and desire isn't coming back?

What if it seems like a permanent condition no matter what efforts are made?

There is a possibility that you or your partner are replaying scripts from your childhood with no conscious awareness of it. Because it's not conscious, it can be difficult to identify, much less communicate. You might say (and truly believe) the reason for your low desire is daily stress, and you may determine all kinds of reasons that vary by the day. You're too hot, you just ate, you're tired from a long day, you're worried the kids will walk in, you need a shower. These reasons can be legitimate and make sense in the moment, but they can also be defenses meant to disguise, even from yourself, the real source of your avoidance.

As I mentioned previously, we all receive damaging messages about sex throughout our lives, and these messages become beliefs that influence our behavior. It might seem unlikely to you or your partner that you're being influenced by these messages, especially because you would reject them in a second if they were made conscious. Most of us would never say to our partner: "Not tonight babe, on some level I believe if I can't perfectly please you, I'm not a real man." And yet, when our partner initiates sex, a sudden urge to zone out in front of the tv before going to sleep or remembering the phone call we need to make takes over. Unfortunately, and however commonplace, this is a convenient facade for the limiting belief. Instead of interrogating the feeling, we say we're tired or we say we're stressed. It may be true, but it isn't the complete story.

For example, Jeff, a loving and supportive husband and playful dad, stopped feeling aroused by his wife after they got married and has no idea why. For years, he's blamed it on low libido. He couldn't truly suffer low libido though, because he is aroused by pornographic images of women in BDSM scenarios, something he feels deep guilt about and hides from his wife. He doesn't realize that when he was young, he internalized a belief that sex is deviant, and that to remain worthy of love, he should hide any sexual feelings from his family. This followed a childish misconception based on his mother's reactions that if he acted out, she would suffer physical pain.

Jeff would never say to himself: "I can't have sex with a woman I love and respect because wanting a bad thing like sex makes me unworthy of love." Or: "I can only feel aroused by women who don't care if I cause them physical pain." But the core belief has a stronghold. So much so that the moment he married his wife and they became each other's family, he could no longer feel desire for her. His unconscious fear that he will hurt the person he loves, along with anxiety that she will stop loving him for being "bad," means he can only respond sexually to fantasies of "deviant" women with whom he has no connection and could "hurt" without consequence. When his wife initiates, he feels anxious. He's come to dread her invitations and shuts down when she tries to talk to him about it.

Attachment Style

It's helpful to consider your relationship to your parents and your early childhood experiences. The most powerful messages we get about physical intimacy and the nature of our bodies come from our earliest days with our caretakers. How often our parents gave us affection, whether or not they affirmed the joy we took in our physical sensations, how they regarded our bodies, and whether or not they welcomed our autonomy all inform our comfort level with the act of sex and the relationships we have with our sexual partners.

If, as a toddler, your mother swatted your hand away and said "No!" when you were curious about your genitals, you might feel conflicted when your genitals respond to arousal or your partner's touch. This is related to "Attachment Theory," and the attachment style you developed in response to your caretaker's behavior accounts for some of your habits in relationships. For example, if you usually felt safe in your father's arms and equally safe to leave his lap and play, you probably have a secure attachment style and don't have difficulty being intimate with a partner. On the other hand, if your parents worried when you toddled off and routinely pulled you back, or if they harshly scolded you when you made a mess exploring, you probably have an insecure attachment style. Because your early explorations of the world were considered dangerous and destructive, you might shut down when your partner wants to explore your sexual relationship. If a parent or caregiver was inconsistently responsive to your needs, or perhaps unpredictable in their moods or actions, you learned that you couldn't rely on them and that needing someone was a weakness and, as a result, you might feel resentful of your partner for needing you.

You needed to feel free and unselfconscious when you broke away from your caregiver. You needed not to worry that your caregiver would be upset when you returned to them. You needed them to welcome you back and positively reflect the joy you took in your adventures. You needed to be sure you were still loved when you were apart from them. You needed to learn that you could carry the image of them with you and also that they kept you inside of them while you were gone from each other. A caregiver who was angry at you for wandering off made you feel smothered, but their anger warned you to sacrifice your need for autonomy and to stay close. A caregiver who was distant when you returned and too preoccupied by their own interests awakened abandonment fears, and though you longed to go play, you stayed close to make sure *they* didn't leave *you*.

As an adult, you may have a partner who is belligerent or hostile when you have to separate from them and while you may resent this, on a deeper level you fear that your independence makes you unlovable. Or you may have a partner who takes no notice of your comings and goings and you feel anxious about their ambivalence; you might beg them to put the phone down, stop working so much, stop letting everything else consume them. In either case, when your partner isn't a safe base from which you can freely leave and be welcomed back, you cannot experience the vulnerability of emotional intimacy with them, nor can you travel to the unselfconscious zone of sexual intimacy. You will either feel forced to regulate your partner's mood by giving up your own needs, or you will feel insecure about your partner's devotion and spend considerable energy trying to secure their attention. In either case, you will be trading your need for autonomy for your need for safety when a healthy relationship requires both, as well as: a sense of belonging, emotional validation, and physical touch. These are things we cannot provide ourselves and are dependent on others to provide.

It's funny that it seems we can ignore our internalized beliefs for a while when our relationships are new, or before we fully commit to our partners. There is something about transitioning from two independent people to a family of two that seems to shake loose the drama of our childhood and compels us to repeat patterns from our earliest experiences. I believe it's our desire for healing. Unconsciously, we see our partners as our caregiver and protector and want them to help us revisit and recover from past pain. We want them to give us the attention and affirmation we needed but didn't get from our original caretakers. Our partners *can* help us accomplish these goals, but first, we need to figure out what we've locked away and why-- then open the door and let our partner in.

The Uncertainty of Relationships

Let me go ahead and put this out there: relationships are fragile. That may seem obvious, but we don't act like it. We tend to believe that the longer we're together and the more we've invested in our shared life, the safer we are. We think sharing bills or kids is proof that our partner's devotion is binding. We put faith in our marriage vows, hoping we'll be the successful half of divorce statistics. We know if nothing else, the legal agreement of marriage implies a penalty for its dissolution, and our partner probably wishes to avoid that headache as much as we do. Adding to this certainty is the fact that part of our identity comes from our relationship to each other; we see ourselves as so-and-so's wife or husband and offer this as our title to the outside world. We're anchored to this role, just as we are to the roles of father, mother, son or daughter.

Because we take each other's presence in our lives as a given, we don't extend resources to keep each other interested. Instead, we conserve our energy. Complacent, we turn our attention to other matters. While this energy conservation makes sense--after all, we are limited in how much we have available to commit--it poses a substantial threat to the relationship we feel secure enough to ignore.

The fact is, we cannot control our partners any more than we can control the rotation of the earth. And there is no insurance policy against outside threats to our relationship. Our partners are autonomous beings. They have singular experiences, independent thoughts, and may hide parts of themselves, either to escape the relationship or to accommodate it. They might betray us, lie to us, or leave us. Understandably, we want to avoid the anxiety of this inconvenient truth, and it makes sense that we would rely on the construct of monogamy as a guarantee. And while we can feel justified in our *expectation* of reliability--our partner did commit themselves to us--ultimately, our partner is not a trophy we won, nor can we keep them locked inside a cage. They actively *choose* to be with us each day...the door to the cage stands wide open. With that in mind, I urge you to be proactive and protective. Pay attention to it. Make it a priority.

Be the guardian of your intimate life.

I've seen too many couples half-heartedly commit to improve their intimacy, often to their ultimate downfall. I've seen too many individuals dismiss their partner's need for intimate connection, failing to recognize how they've forsaken them. There are no guarantees in life, but you have a fighting chance at lasting love if you nurture your intimate connection. This book will give you the tools to do just that.

THE MIND-BODY CONNECTION

THE 4 INTIMACY STYLES

Chapter 4
Defining Intimacy

The Importance of Physical Intimacy

Intimacy can mean a lot of things. It can describe the safety and attachment you feel in a familiar relationship, the deep knowledge you have of either a friend or a partner, or it can describe the exclusive and cozy mood of dinner by candlelight. It can also be understood as a euphemism for sexual intercourse. But while intimacy can be another word for sex, sex can sometimes be anything but intimate. Sometimes it's anything but familiar, as with a new partner, and sometimes it's tedious, boring, uninspired...maybe even painful. When we were young and sexually inexperienced, many of us dreamed of our eventual sexual encounters and believed they would be otherworldly, full of passion, and of course, intimate. No one ever told us sex could sometimes be the opposite.

If the sex you're having is like this or happening so infrequently it isn't anything at all, the root cause is--you guessed it--the lack of intimacy. So, what can you do? Intimacy isn't something you can summon from thin air. It may take a long time, even if you're rebuilding from a previously strong intimacy that has now faded.

Oftentimes couples will start with emotional intimacy, connecting through communication and caring gestures, but sometimes the opposite works too; experimenting with physical intimacy can often be the path to experiencing emotional intimacy. I have worked with so many individuals and couples who have shared that connecting physically either sparked or heightened their emotional connection. They report to me that through physical vulnerability, they feel they share a sacred piece of themselves reserved for each other, and that this forms the basis of their emotional connection.

Sexual Boundaries

Healthy sexual exploration can't take place without boundaries. It cannot happen until we ask ourselves the questions "what do I want" and "what don't I want." Without those answers, we will lack fundamental emotional and physical intimacy. It's simply impossible to know our partner without knowing their limits.

There is no doubt we foster intimacy with our partner when we make ourselves vulnerable and communicate with them directly. But no amount of clearing the air or avoiding harmful dynamics will be possible until both you and your partner have a clear understanding of what sexual intimacy means to you and how you want it to show up in your relationship. Many couples are familiar with the "Defining the Relationship Talk," but few define the terms *sex* and *intimacy* with their partners.

Knowing your own body, where you like to be touched, and how you like to engage in sexual activity is useful. But being able to talk about it is much more important. Why?

No good sex partner will want to do something you don't feel comfortable doing.

When you can't or won't talk about your experience and your preferences, it can come across as if you don't know what you like or you're not okay with what you're doing, and neither inspires confidence in your partner. If you don't know what you want, you can't rely on your partner to help you figure it out. Even though you and your partner *will* discover new preferences with time and experimentation, you still need to identify your sexual boundaries. Without them, you will experience disappointing sex and there's no reason you or your partner should have to accept that.

Individuals who do not know what they like or what they're okay with sexually, do not have good sexual boundaries. This lack of self-knowledge carries some amount of risk as well because it opens up the possibility of experiencing something very unpleasant and possibly traumatic. I'm not saying it's necessary to know *everything* you enjoy. But it's important to have a starting point to know enough about what you do and do not like in order to give your partner some guidance.

For some, giving free rein to sexual partners might feel exciting, or perhaps easier. Even in this scenario, understanding your own body is helpful. Self-touch can help you establish what sensations bring you the most pleasure and how to stimulate them without the distraction or "busy" feeling of a partnered experience.

Taking time to explore your own body through self-touch is the key to better sex with your partner.

Your partner may not be able to perfectly simulate what you do on your own, but they can come very close if you understand where on your body you like to be touched, and what amount of pressure, frequency, or combination of sensations you enjoy. As the owner of your body and your sexuality, it is up to you to set the boundaries for any partner. Knowing and sharing your sexual boundaries will help your partner know how to play with you without fear of rejection. Remember that good sex partners not only respect your boundaries, but they also want to know that the experience is pleasurable for both of you.

Sexual Pleasure

Among sexologists, it's a widely held belief that "sex is how adults play." And just like play was more fun with other kids growing up, sexual play is better when it's not a solitary endeavor. Sex isn't much of an adventure if you always anticipate your next move.

What's interesting about partnered sex is you can experience as much pleasure giving it to your partner as you would receiving it. What's more, depending on your Intimacy Style, you might like to experience intimacy in a way that differs from how you express it. For example, you might be the type of person who gets turned on when your partner tells you all the juicy details about how they want to be intimate but find it exceptionally uncomfortable to even think about "talking dirty." You might instead get an equal amount of pleasure from letting your body do all the talking. But to experience pleasure at all, you first need to feel safe.

When we played as children, we felt only as free to imagine and create as we felt certain our caregivers would be there to welcome us back to reality. The less certain our attachment, the less we were able to untether ourselves to explore our fantasy worlds. Survival is our first instinct and because we depended on our caretakers, their support made all the difference in whether or not we felt secure enough to fully and enthusiastically express ourselves. We would "check-in," every now and then by searching for our caretaker's face to make eye contact, and eye contact returned from them was our go-ahead. The quality of support we receive from our partners now is what determines our ability to play; they are the safe base from which we leave and come back. Seeking our partner through sex to confirm that they're there, and it's ok to play may not necessarily involve eye contact if we're in a dark room or we're not face-to-face. As such, it's so important to resolve each other's need to safely explore by making our sex life a zone of no judgement, where we give to each other freely and we're open to experimentation. Sex is a venue to access not only our imagination and fantasy, but the intimacy of knowing each other, and knowing we're safe and have the freedom to explore. As Plato said, "you can discover more about a person in an hour of play than in a year of conversation."

There is no one-size-fits-all when it comes to sexual pleasure, but it is safe to say that consent and expressed desire for sex adds to the mutual pleasure of a sexual interaction. And then there's reckless abandon. There have been countless instances of me explaining to my clients that sex should be something to look back on with a smile or even a laugh. And, if you're doing it right, you may even experience a tinge of embarrassment recalling your lack of inhibition.

Pleasure lives in between self-awareness and partner-awareness.

Pleasure lives somewhere between wanting to take and wanting to be taken. It requires you to check your day-to-day identities at the bedroom door and set down the loads of obligation and caretaking. You cannot be stimulated by or stimulating to your partner unless you occupy your own pleasure and stay there, feeling and owning your sensations. Pleasure is freedom and surrender. Pleasure transforms the nature of our intimate connection; with pleasure, sex is not a chore. It becomes a sacred space we occupy where time, duty, and other people's needs don't exist. It is simply us taking pleasure from our partner and our partner taking pleasure from us.

In our quest for pleasure, it is important to remember we are carnal beings with a physical body, and we come equipped with all the bodily systems that keep us alive, all the requirements such as food or water, and all the experiences that activate through brain chemistry and blood flow. We were made to feel cold in freezing temperatures, pain when we are hurt, hungry when we need to eat, and pleasure in the act of sex. Pleasure is a gift of our biology that allows us to experience, among other things, a deep connection with our sexual partners. There is a purpose to pleasure and the role it plays. It is not an accident that the basic function of sex also bonds us to the person we engage in it with. We are meant to access pleasure through our partners and meant to experience it together. Even though we will not die without it, the pleasure of sex and the appetite that motivates us to seek it out surely helped to guarantee the survival of our species.

That said, despite it being "natural" there is nothing wrong with you if you have difficulty accessing pleasure. The problem is not with you, but with a cultural narrative that offers a very narrow path you're meant to carefully tread. As I discussed in Chapter 1, damaging messages from a lifetime of socialization are a powerful opponent of nature. We couldn't shut down our breathing if society told us it was untoward, and society can't fully condemn the act of sex since it creates families, but pleasure is neither automatic nor does it serve a function that benefits society, so on the chopping block it goes. Our culture is anti-pleasure, sexual or otherwise. We're taught that suffering and hard work are virtues, and pleasure and self-gratification are vices. We have all learned to deny our longing for pleasure and hide the rare moments we do experience it. But I would argue that pleasure in one's body and passion for one's partner is an investment in physical and mental health and an investment in long-term monogamy, and both of these benefit the family unit which benefits the community.

I also believe human beings are made to experience joy and connection; really, to express the universe's joy of creation. We're the only species that can make narrative sense of our experiences and in that way, pleasure becomes a story we share. Pleasure informs our fantasies, and it is through fantasy that we can find new levels to pleasure. As children we had playmates with who we sought day after day to escape into imaginary landscapes; as adults our playmates are our partners, and we invite them to co-create a plot. Our creative drive transforms sex from something all other mammals do to reproduce, to something uniquely human and uniquely intimate.

Sexual Variety & Frequency

When working with couples, I inevitably get asked the million-dollar question: ***How often should we be having sex?*** Let's break down that question. When a couple asks about "shoulds," they're really asking, "Are we okay?" They want to diagnose themselves by comparing their sexual frequency to an average but, ultimately, couples aren't aspiring to be normal. They want to be *better* than normal, and more than okay. They want to be (or become) a *good* statistic. So, they implore me to rate them on a scale, and hope I give them the secret to boosting their numbers.

Technically, the clinical definition of a sexless marriage is one in which sexual intimacy occurs less than 10 times a year, but I believe the quality of the intimacy and the couple's satisfaction is what matters. Couples could engage in sexual intimacy 10 times a week and still feel there's something amiss in the quality of their intimacy. And because we aren't machines, I don't recommend a specific number of times a couple should have intercourse, but I do recommend at least two instances of sexual play per week.

While even the busiest of couples can manage to make time for two sessions of sexual intercourse per week, intercourse is not the only sexual play that matters. Any kind of sensual activity is relevant here. Massages, cuddling, brushing your partner's hair, showering together--even sending a simple "sext"--all of these count. I suggest couples aim to have sexual intercourse at least once weekly, but the other activity they choose does not have to be elaborate and can remain purely sensual. Anything to inject a sexual or sensual mood into your week is compatible with the goals of this recommendation. Think of it like self-care, because it is. Yes, it benefits your partner, but by making sexual connection a practice, you are essentially making space in your life to feel pleasure, and to feel cared for. You're also prioritizing your relationship which means you don't have to feel guilty for neglecting it. Guilt is so corrosive to intimacy because it activates that good ol' evolutionary stress response and makes you feel unsafe.

*Feeling unsafe about intimacy
is the quickest way to shut it down.*

Sometimes self-care amounts to doing what you know needs to be done to create balance in your mood and environment, and in order to feel safe again. It is present-you taking care of future-you. It may seem impossible or inconvenient to clear time in your schedule to exercise, but once you do you feel so much better. It's not pleasurable or fun, but washing the dishes and clearing the counter before bed means you wake up to a clean kitchen. Making lunches the night before, gives you a few minutes to make your beloved tea or coffee in the morning. Sensual and sexual activity, while hopefully more enticing than dishes or the treadmill, is the same. It may be hard to work up to, it may feel like it's taking time from something else, you may be left hot and sweaty. But there's no denying the endorphins you feel and the stress relief it provides. There's no denying that feeling close to your partner beats feeling estranged. Harmony in your relationship infuses your body, mind, and living space with peace. There's no candle or bubble bath on the market that can do that, no matter what their labels claim.

Foreplay Starts Outside The Bedroom

When a couple is not on the same page about the significance of sexuality in their relationship it can create a chasm between them. Usually this results in the couple pretending the chasm is non-existent in the hope that it will seal up on its own. In the previous chapter, I explained that passive body language informs your partner minute-to-minute whether you desire them or not. I also stressed that feeling desired by one's partner is a powerful and universal need. The way you joke about sexuality in passing, the way you touch your partner (or abstain from touching your partner), the looks you give each other...all communicate your level of sexual interest or apathy.

I'll let you in on a well-known secret within the sex therapy community: foreplay starts outside the bedroom and long before the sex act itself. In fact, as I often tell clients, seduction begins immediately following the end of your last sexual experience. This is especially true for women, who can experience arousal as intensely as men but usually need more warming up, both physically, as a lead up to intercourse, and mentally and emotionally, throughout the day. This can be a difficult concept for both men and women to appreciate because in our culture we're socialized to see arousal as spontaneous; something that "just happens." This can be a destructive myth because if you or your partner do not experience desire at the very thought of sex, you may believe there's something wrong with you. Let me assure you, you are completely normal--5% of men and 30% of women do not experience spontaneous desire--and whether or not you need stimulation to experience desire may be dictated by your Intimacy Style. There are also people (many of whom also fit in the above category) who experience contextual desire which means they need to be in a certain place, have certain conditions met, or be in a certain frame of mind before they feel aroused. So, if the experience of spontaneous desire doesn't describe what happens with you or your partner, it helps to see foreplay as a long, drawn-out process that starts as soon as you wake up each day.

Foreplay is getting your partner a cup of coffee while they're still in bed. It's advancing the laundry when they're preoccupied and forgot about the soccer uniform that needs to be clean and dry by this evening. It's filling their car with gas when you realize they're low (and maybe grabbing some of their favorite snacks while you're there). It's watching a movie they've been dying to see but thought you wouldn't be into. In this way, you stoke your interactions and build a slow burn over hours, even days. These interactions should be filled with generosity: be compassionate toward your partner, compliment them, and appreciate what they do for you. Be affectionate. Kiss each other. *Not pecks.* Full on passionate kissing that accelerates your heart rate.

——————— *Think about it:* ———————

For partners who are experiencing desire discrepancy, kissing or making out can sometimes feel threatening to the partner who wants less sex.

They may feel it's expected of them to "go all the way." This conflict between what they want and what they think is expected of them can trigger that damning evolutionary "freeze" response, which will (of course) lead to them clamming up. It may not feel romantic to explain the terms of this make-out session, but it will likely help your partner feel more at ease and then relax enough to fully enjoy it. You can even take ownership with an I-statement and say, "I don't want to have sex, I just want to kiss you." Explicitly "calling your shot" so to speak, spares your partner the anxiety of not knowing what will happen, or the feeling that they're not in control. Just make sure to keep your word, or else you could lose trust.

At the same time, it's important to understand that the nuance of desire demands a negotiation between focused devotion (all those kind and romantic gestures) and flirty nonchalance. Our partners cannot be drawn to us if we're always underfoot or constantly appeasing them like a servant. Our partners feel the most compelled by us when they see us confidently take charge of what needs to be done without waiting for their approval or assistance. When we were first dating our partner (in the era of the instinctive and intense desire), we hadn't yet combined our lives, nor were we interdependent in any significant way. Our partner was not aware of when our bills were due, or if we had a lightbulb that needed changing. They didn't know if we were low on milk or if we had strong opinions about bedtime temperature. And while it's true that we can't reclaim our mystery in the realm of household habits, we *can* be less dependent on our partner. There's nothing sexier than a partner who wants us but does not need us. On the contrary, a partner who is needy and insecure is a partner that triggers us to comfort them. When we nurture like this, we are intimate with our partners, but it can feel like we're caring for a child--and that is decidedly *not* a turn-on. Pre-bedroom foreplay should involve loving kindness *without* neediness. We should take on a confident but companionable air that says, "I don't need you here, but I'm happy that you are." In this context, sex may not "just happen," but the anticipation for it will build so much that by the time it does, it will be fulfilling to you both.

THE 4 INTIMACY STYLES

Chapter 5
A Case of Sexual Disconnect

What about when one partner gets weighed down in life's demands and prioritizes anything and everything over sex, while the other partner highly values their sexual intimacy and considers it a high priority?

CASE STUDY:

Meet James and Nykeisha

James and Nykeisha have been married for 6 years, together for 8. They have two children under the age of 5. In their courtship years, sex was impassioned and frequent, but tapered off after they were married. After having the kids, it dwindled to once, maybe twice a month. They would both like to have more sex, but James is far more invested in this goal than Nykeisha.

James believes if his wife stopped putting sex on the back burner, their intimacy troubles would be eliminated. Nykeisha, who knowingly assigns greater importance to daily tasks, feels if she doesn't take care of the hard stuff, no one will. Nykeisha wishes James understood how hard it is to switch off the "family manager" part of her brain. Nykeisha schedules every appointment, pays every bill, runs most of the household errands, and acts as the primary contact for their children's daycare, the soccer coach, the pediatrician, the repairmen and pest control, as well as all of their extended family. There is always shopping to do, meals to be cooked, birthday parties to RSVP to, and piles of laundry to deal with, which Nykeisha feels certain are invisible to James. The less James sees or appreciates Nykeisha's efforts, the less Nykeisha wants to have sex. The less Nykeisha wants to have sex, the more desperate James feels. They're at a stalemate.

James believes he has a high sex drive and that Nykeisha has low sexual desire, and wonders if they have a physiological incompatibility. Mismatched sexual desire doesn't always result from an actual, physical discrepancy; it can sometimes more accurately be described as "mismatched interest." But there are dozens of physical causes for loss of desire, and these should always be ruled out by a health professional. This has become a point of contention for James and Nykeisha, as James has urged Nykeisha to see a doctor several times, and Nykeisha keeps putting it off. James feels unloved as the days go by and she still won't schedule an appointment. He believes she's sending a message that his needs are not important to her.

Meanwhile, Nykeisha feels justified focusing her attention on the juggling act of adult responsibility, in fact, she finds it crucial. By comparison, she admits she doesn't find James' desire for more sex all that pressing and believes he can and should accept her disinterest...for better or for worse, right?

A CASE OF SEXUAL DISCONNECT

She also feels "touched out" most days after all the physical contact she has with their young children and just wants to be left alone. The last thing she needs is someone else climbing on her. Something she's less aware of is how her own needs for intimacy, physical touch, and affection are met by the children, leaving her husband's touch irrelevant. She and James routinely argue these points and she feels resentful that he doesn't seem to recognize how exhausted she is. James feels frustrated by what he considers an excuse to avoid intimacy.

Every once in a while, Nykeisha gives in to James, but while her body is in the act, her mind is on the grocery list. James can sense that she's distracted and loses interest as well as his erection. He's embarrassed by this, but he'd rather be celibate than feel he's forcing sex on his indifferent wife.

Meanwhile, the household chores accumulate and make their way onto Nykeisha's to-do list each day, and each of them seem more urgent to her than spicing up her marriage. She says it might be nice for James to take some of the load off of her; maybe then she'd be more relaxed and want to jump into bed. James hears this complaint and tries to do his part to take the kids so she gets time to herself and does more of his fair share of the housework. He's willing to do anything, and each day hopes that she notices the effort he's making. After two weeks of doing as much sweeping and laundering as he can, he asks for sex and he's turned down. Nykeisha says her day was long and she feels worn out. "Maybe this weekend?" she says, before rolling over in bed and scrolling her phone. James says nothing, just gets up and goes to watch tv in another room.

It's easy to see how both James and Nykeisha are feeding into the conflict, how their feelings and points of view are both valid, and why they both feel unheard and unseen. Their situation is common--it's a dynamic I see over and over again. Because I'm a sex therapist, and physical intimacy is a common goal of my clients, I would want to find a way to make sure Nykeisha felt validated by her husband, then explore her reluctance in an atmosphere of safety and low conflict. The safety would extend to James, to explore his feelings of lowered confidence from repeated sexual rejection. Hopefully, we would find the problem within the problem, as most of these conflicts have hidden roots under the surface. It isn't as simple as James taking more of the household burden and Nykeisha giving in to his requests. We know from their story that Nykeisha occasionally will have sex with James but it's unsatisfying for them both. And when James makes more of an effort to relieve Nykeisha, she still turns him down.

——————— *Think about it:* ———————

What's really at work here? With whom do
you most relate to in this case study?

A CASE OF SEXUAL DISCONNECT

THE 4 INTIMACY STYLES

Chapter 6
Our Partner Isn't the Enemy

The Importance of Trust

During the process of creating emotional and/or physical intimacy, trust has to be rebuilt. Lack of trust causes a feedback loop: without sufficient trust in the relationship, there won't be any trust in the bedroom; without trust in the bedroom, the relationship will suffer. In this environment, couples have difficulty discussing even the simplest of relational issues for fear that it will be taken personally, or that their pride will be bruised. Distrust threatens their equilibrium and with it goes their desire. Without the foundation of trust, they will never be able to relax and let go enough to experience physical intimacy or develop emotional intimacy.

Trust is what allows us to function in our lives.

It is the basic premise that what we expect to happen will happen. The day will dawn, the train will come, the clock will report the correct time, the grocery store will stock what we need. We rely on the order of things to make us feel safe, to enable us to take risks within their boundaries and accept the unknown. Without trust in our surroundings, we would be paralyzed, unable to live moment to moment. We would be unable to risk love, afraid we would suffer loss.

This is not a far-off reality for couples struggling with trust. These couples will treat each other as potential enemies and focus on each other's flaws to such an extent that they cannot see or admit that their partner possesses positive traits. Even when their partner says or does something to support them or the relationship there is still an outcry. "Why now?" "Why didn't you do this before?" Without trust, it is impossible to believe their partner's intentions are good and it feels safer to shield themselves from being hurt by constructing an impenetrable wall of anger, or to strike first with criticism. These partners will refuse to let their guard down by so much as smiling or accepting a compliment. Their underlying resentment is a strict monitor, warning them to never seem satisfied lest they be taken advantage of. Under these conditions, intimacy is impossible. Intimacy is the very opposite of distrust.

It is a common belief that reciprocity is the engine of trust, as it accomplishes the mutual goals of both parties. In other words, if I do something for you, you now have to do something for me. We both get something we want or need, and now we know we can rely on each other. Within the context of a relationship, this seems like a good strategy, but couples who exchange favors this way are operating on a well-intentioned but flawed premise. When partners don't have the same love language, an even trade is impossible to transact. Dr. Gary Chapman, the author of *The Five Love Languages: The Secret to Love that Lasts* explains that as individuals we have our own unique emotional language which determines how we express and receive love, and if our partner's language differs from our own, we may find that our expressions of love fall on deaf ears. We make a sincere effort and get very little or no acknowledgment from our partner. As Dr. Chapman writes, "We are expressing love, but the message does not come through because we are speaking what, to them, is a foreign language." The concept of love languages shows that if partners expect to receive an equivalent action of kindness from each other to return one of their own, they have a long wait with no guarantee, during which time resentment and distrust will build. These couples will end up keeping score, a practice that severely undermines trust.

The feeling of being left out to dry, or the feeling that your partner routinely takes from you but doesn't give, can make your efforts feel cheap, and leave you feeling used and foolish for trusting them. In this climate, a spirit of goodwill feels too vulnerable. You might worry you will be taken advantage of and withdraw any favors or help, or vow to stop relying on them for their help, leaving you both stranded on separate emotional islands. This is the dynamic of partners who keep a running tally of who owes whom for what and how much.

The running tally is really a test couples subject each other to, and it's a familiar test of general social interaction. The test is made up of one question: *will you honor your commitment to me?* In our lives, we have plenty of opportunity to judge the trustworthiness of others through their actions, and we do so on a subconscious level. In our relationships with friends, family, coworkers, supervisors and so on, we stay apprised of how overall trustworthy they are by observing their behavior. If they make it to the meeting on time, we mentally add this to the trustworthy column. If they forget to call when they said they would, it gets added to the untrustworthy column. Our brain logs the information and we do the math. If someone who ordinarily comes through for us doesn't on occasion, we don't worry because we have a backlog of data that shows this person to be reliable; a "cushion" that prevents us from smacking into the floor. Similarly, the individual with more bulk in the untrustworthy column doesn't surprise us when they don't follow through. These scenarios are predictable and don't necessarily trigger our anxiety but when our partner's behavior shows up in the untrustworthy column, we panic. Yet losing trust in a partner happens quickly and easily. And the commitments we expect them to honor are much stricter and sometimes abstract. We feel suspicious when they're distracted or when they have complaints because on some basic level, we expect our partners to make us the center of their worlds and see us as blameless. When we realize our marriage and our partner are both imperfect, it awakens our fears of abandonment.

Accepting that our partner will not always anticipate our needs or behave as we want them to is difficult, but important to rebuilding trust.

And switching to a charitable mindset when our fears are aroused may feel impossible. But when you practice helping your partner without expectation of return or reward, you create a culture of respect and generosity. By striving to do the right thing (when you know what the right thing is), you can look at yourself in the mirror and know that you are a good partner. Committing two wrongs only means you have to avoid your reflection, and it certainly won't help the relationship.

We tend to have an easier time offering generosity and respect to friends, coworkers, and our children; we're more forgiving and we offer more chances. In some cases, as with children, we're free to simply enjoy them. We understand we can't expect reciprocity, and we're happy to support them without emotional compensation. And in the case of adult acquaintances and friends, coworkers, supervisors, clients, etc., a funny and inverse phenomenon occurs: we are our best selves for them. For them we are cheerful, helpful, and understanding. We commit to their goals, ideas, needs, well-being, and happiness. Because of course, if a client is unhappy with us, we might lose them. If a friend is hurt by us, they might withdraw their friendship. Somehow, we don't appreciate the fact that if our partner is dissatisfied, we may also lose them. And yet the fear of losing them is often the motive behind our negative behavior. I can see in the couples I work with that they know the loss of their partner is a possibility. Both parties will struggle to openly share their contribution to the dysfunction in their relationship because they fear it will build their partner's case against them and cause them to leave.

But if you decide to enter into the same social contract with your partner as you would any other important person in your life and work to develop a culture of respect, you will find the fear of abandonment is overshadowed by a desire to sustain your partner. It will be difficult to find fault with them when you invest in their well-being the way you would a friend. It will be easier to believe your partner is trying their best and to meet them where they are. When you stop fighting for fairness, and instead fight for your partner, you will find that you care less about what you are entitled to in the relationship, and more about the meaning and purpose of the relationship. We can only assign meaning to our relationships when we feel worthwhile as people, and to decide for yourself that with or without your partner's approval, you matter and your relationship matters. This will mean you are truly able to extend grace to your partner because they're also a part of the relationship; they matter too.

The irony is, by removing the expectation of reciprocity and trusting your partner, your partner is naturally inclined to return your unselfishness. They will trust *you* more, as they feel liberated from the rigid rules of score keeping. This is how intimacy is built: through kind, thoughtful, and selfless acts of care, and through trusting that if you open up to your partner, they will be available for you. It only takes one partner to commit to this course of action for both partners to feel safe within the relationship.

Initiating is a Trust Fall

The topic of initiation comes up in almost all my work with couples. In most long-term relationships, a dynamic emerges where one partner initiates most of the time, leaving the other partner to make the call and decide what they'll be doing (or not doing) for the next half hour at least. One partner takes on the risk and the other has the power. It's easy to see how this dynamic causes friction. To add to the confusion, I often hear from women who say that they feel like they *shouldn't* be the initiator and from men, that they have felt burdened by the task. Regardless, the partner who initiates may always have done so or partners may trade this role back and forth, but, generally speaking, the initiating partner is the one who's more motivated by sex. Why specifically they're motivated will be determined by their Intimacy Style; some want closeness, some want validation, others simply need that release. If their initiation strategy typically works well and they feel their partner generally accepts their requests, they won't mind performing this role. But when the initiator's strategies typically *don't* work, intimacy suffers and resentment grows. In this case, the initiator is racked with doubt as their thoughts race: "Does she seem like she wants to have sex right now? Will he say no? Is the timing right? Am I getting my point across or am I being too subtle? Am I being too demanding? Why doesn't he desire me? I want her so much." Sometimes these thoughts are self-defeating ("She'll only say no," or "It'll only cause a fight") and the initiation never happens. What should be a fun, flirty, and intimate connection turns into a heartbreaking ritual of yearning, worry, negative self-talk, and finally despair.

The partner who decides, decides for them both. He or she determines the frequency of their sex life, which can ultimately determine the overall quality and satisfaction. They are making a decision that impacts them both, but in the moment, this partner is only thinking, "Do *I* want to?" And that makes sense. Something is being offered. When a friend offers us a drink, we don't think to ourselves, "Would having a drink benefit *us*?" We consider our own appetite for it. We consider our own enjoyment of the experience. And if we turn it down, our friend is not offended, much less hurt. The only difference is the drink is not shared...it is not "ours," it is "mine." By turning it down we are not also taking away *their* option to have a drink--they get to have the experience they're offering us, with or without us.

*Because sex is shared, two rules
need to be in place, and they
may seem contradictory:
consent and compromise.*

Consent is nonnegotiable--it is the foundation of any positive sexual interaction. No partner should ever be pressured, guilted, coerced, or criticized into having sex. Not only is it abusive to subject your partner to these tactics, he or she cannot relax and enjoy sex under those conditions. Compromise is also necessary, so if a couple is chronically at odds with their degree of intimacy, they need to develop a game plan. I'll get to that in a moment.

─────── *Think about it:* ───────

How long can a couple go on if one of them
has a need that is inconsistently or almost
never met by their partner? How long can
the partner turning down intimacy withstand
the guilt and pressure they experience?

I often tell my non-initiating clients that if their partner is a good person, before long, it will feel like they are doing something *to* them, not *with* them. How much risk can the initiator take, and how many rejections can they suffer before their trust in their partner is gone? Initiation is a trust fall. How many times can someone fall on their back when they believed their partner was waiting to catch them? And how can someone be a soft landing if they anticipate being crushed?

Communication in the Pursuer-Distancer Model

The initiator vs. decider dynamic creates a breeding ground for misunderstandings, lack of confidence (leading to lack of clarity), guilt, shame, rejection, self-doubt, and frustration. You might be able to express to your partner what you need from them emotionally with absolute certainty and ease, but when it comes to sex, you feel paralyzed. Without communication, the initiator and decider can get locked into what is known as "pursuer-distancer" roles.

Pursuers tend to, well, pursue. In emotional matters, the pursuer is after conflict resolution, and their strategy is to nag their partner. Why would they nag if all they want is peace? Well, because they're reacting to the distancer. While the pursuer is alert to problems within the relationship and pokes and prods their partner, the distancer is withdrawn. They are shut down-- absent both mentally and emotionally. This is unbearable to the pursuer, who needs a lot of reassuring touch and communication in order to feel secure. As their anxiety grows, the pursuer puts more pressure on the distancer. The added pressure suffocates and overwhelms the distancer, who retreats even more. Thus, they bob and weave in an endless match that yields no winner, and has no referee.

In the sexual arena, pursuers are the initiators and the distancers reject their advances. Sometimes the pursuer is aggressive and critical and sometimes they're clingy, but none of this behavior moves the distancer, who barely acknowledges their attempts. The distancer feels that their partner is never satisfied, and they resent feeling as though they're constantly being asked to take care of their needs. At some point, exhausted by their efforts, the pursuer gives up and becomes equally withdrawn. Pursuing sex with their detached partner has become too much of an emotional risk. The same weary détente can happen in an emotional pursuer-distancer dynamic. These pursuer-partners who give up forfeit their emotional and/or sexual connection, and soon these couples find themselves living as roommates.

In the same relationship, there may be one partner who plays the pursuer role in emotional matters, while the other plays the pursuer in their sex life. In the field of psychotherapy and couples counseling there is a common belief that emotional pursuers are women, and sexual pursuers are men. In the emotional paradigm this would mean the woman overwhelms her male partner with relational "flooding" and he shuts down in response. In the sexual paradigm, this would look like a male pursuer nagging his female distancer partner with an avalanche of requests for sex that border on begging, while she withdraws into herself. I don't like to make gendered and heteronormative designations in my practice because they are erroneous in my opinion, and largely the result of socialization. The aforementioned gender dynamic may be true to your experience, but in so many cases it is flipped, or occurs between gay, lesbian, and nonbinary partners. You can apply your experience to either role regardless of gender or sexuality, but it's worth noting that we may have these preconceived notions of male/female roles simply because men and women are socialized to perform them. Some will naturally align with these gender norms, but it's possible in some cases that partners are behaving according to what's expected of them, or they self-report that they do (for instance, a woman self-reporting that she is less enthused about sex than her male partner). Same-sex couples have an advantage in this regard, as they are free to choose what roles they play without the constraints of a gendered narrative or society's expectations.

If you are part of a heterosexual couple and you find yourself relating more to behaviors stereotypically associated with the opposite sex, just know that is very common.

Men can very often feel overwhelmed with their female partner's sexual advances, and women can just as commonly feel stifled by their male partner's emotional needs. The stigma that men always want sex and, by contrast, women never or rarely do is harmful to both, particularly in the context of their relationships. A woman who has higher sexual desire than her male partner may feel so abnormal she takes it out on him in an attempt to negate her insecurity and criticizes his lack of desire as being "unmanly." By contrast, he may feel so ineffectual for his lack of desire that he internalizes her attacks and shuts down. There is nothing wrong with either of them, but we haven't allowed enough space in our culture for these identities to thrive.

That said, the idea that there can be a pursuer in the relationship who *only* pursues emotionally but distances sexually, or a distancer in the relationship who avoids sex but tries desperately to connect emotionally is interesting, because it means these two inherently understand each other's position, they just don't realize it. The emotional pursuer, (i.e., the partner that nags to get a response out of the distancer) is trying to alleviate their insecurity. The sexual pursuer, (i.e., the partner that makes repeated attempts to exhort sex) is *also* trying to alleviate their insecurity. These two are playing the same role, just at different times and in different contexts. Perhaps they could consider their partner's behavior in the context of their own. If they did, they might come to the conclusion that their partner is only trying to lessen a feeling of insecurity by prompting their reassurance. Or, as in the case of the sexual distancer rejecting an advance or an emotional distancer shutting down in response to nagging, their partner is flooded, and needs time to process and for them to pull on the reins and go at their partner's pace. These two could try showing each other the compassion *they* need. All they have to do is remember how they feel as either the pursuer or distancer to appreciate their partner's experience. This may also help them appreciate that one of them needs a foundation of emotional intimacy to feel safe being intimate physically, while the other needs physical intimacy to feel validated and confident enough to engage in emotional intimacy.

In the healthiest intimate relationships, couples with opposing Intimacy Styles such as these adopt an egalitarian mindset and agree to a structure that works for them both. They will certainly follow the aforementioned first rule of positive sexual interaction: consent. And they will also abide by the second rule: compromise. They listen to each other's needs and negotiate the details to come up with a mutually satisfying plan. For example, if one partner prefers daytime sex and the other prefers it at bedtime, they might take turns. Or, if one partner finds themselves mentally preoccupied with their to-do list any time their partner "springs sex on them," this couple may agree to schedule sex. I sometimes advise these couples never to reject sexual advances more than twice in a row, a good rule for couples who have reached equilibrium. These couples cannot strike this balance without communication, which may seem obvious, but for couples accustomed to performing pursuer-distancer roles, open communication is terrifying.

Pursuers and distancers are reacting to each other in the biological modality of fight, flight, flee, or freeze. As I brought up in Chapter 3, this evolutionary stress response is a state of hypervigilance, the same as you'd experience if a lurking predator were nearby, so no wonder these two don't feel safe to be vulnerable with each other. In these moments, the neuroanatomist Dr. Jill Bolte Taylor recommends what she calls "the 90-second rule":

> When a person has a reaction to something in their environment, there's a 90-second chemical process that happens in the body; after that, any remaining emotional response is just the person choosing to stay in that emotional loop. Something happens in the external world, and chemicals are flushed through your body which puts it on full alert. For those chemicals to totally flush out of the body, it takes less than 90 seconds. This means that for 90 seconds you can watch the process happening, you can feel it happening, and then you can watch it go away. After that, if you continue to feel fear, anger, and so on, you need to look at the thoughts that you're thinking that are re-stimulating the circuitry that

is resulting in you having this physiological reaction, over and over again.

We don't have to be thoroughly overtaken by our internal alarm system, and, in fact, we aren't wired to be. Our bodies are meant to be alert to the threat and then return to stasis--it's our *thoughts* that keep us in an emotional spiral. This insight offers us tremendous command over our fears. It takes determination and practice, but monitoring and filtering our thoughts is often all that is necessary to break free of the stress that accompanies communication struggles.

Beyond controlling our own thoughts to limit our emotional reactions, it can be helpful to understand two things:

1. Partners in a healthy relationship are also sometimes scared to openly communicate their needs, but they've had enough experience with their partner to realize that if they do it anyway, the nervousness will abate, and the reward will be intimacy.

2. Partners who feel the most desire for each other are skilled at occasionally introducing something new (such as a new way of relating to each other) to the relationship. Sometimes this novelty is as simple as trying a new restaurant together. Sometimes it's about one partner trying something new by themselves and seducing their partner as a bonus, as if to say, "You thought you knew everything about me, but you don't-are you curious to see who I am in this new context?" This is a great way to avoid becoming "that couple" in the restaurant, sitting silently across from each other or lost in their phones. This newness does not always have to be exotic or fun, however. As

counterintuitive and mundane as it might seem, a stab at direct communication can provide the same erotic charge.

Think about it this way: In a business setting, when colleagues are discussing an innovation, there is an energy and excitement in the room (remember: eroticism, or eros, is life pulsing energy). Talking about this new approach makes them eager to start working on it. The same can be true when you raise new concerns or feelings to your partner, as long as you project confidence and don't use the engagement to blame, accuse, criticize, nag, or belittle. You're persuading your partner to try a new dynamic and see how it feels. Persuade comes from the Latin "persuadere" which means "to make sweet for." This is a seduction, not a fight.

If you're the pursuer in the sexual pursuer-distancer dynamic, don't focus on your sexual disconnection, but instead ask them how they would like to reconnect. Rather than say, "You never want to have sex with me," try asking, "How often would you like to have sex?" If you're the distancer in the relationship, tell your partner everything that goes through your mind when they initiate. You will be breaking what your partner perceives as a long and deafening silence and giving them an entry point into understanding you and making sense of your relationship. They will be surprised and touched to discover that you do experience emotions related to this conflict, and they will be eager to hear what those are, even if they don't align with their own. So often, couples learn to live with behavior patterns that they don't even have an explanation for. It's as if they've made an agreement with each other without saying a word. They might know for example that one partner doesn't want sex, but because there was never an explicit conversation about why, both partners are forced to become mind readers and make assumptions about the other's feelings. Neither want to challenge these assumptions because they fear conflict. But buying into assumptions is how the debt of resentment starts to accrue. The only way to clear it is to engage in direct communication.

System of Reward vs. System of Punishment

In addition to the initiator-decider and pursuer-distancer dynamics, I see another common pattern of behavior crop up between partners with ongoing intimacy battles. One of them sees sex as a system of reward and the other sees it as a system of punishment.

For the partner who operates in the system of reward, sex is something they earn. They try to be worthy of their sexual partner by helping them, being nice to them, and offering them gifts and support. There is nothing this partner won't do in order to "win" sex. They usually do not disclose this strategy to their partner because they themselves are barely conscious of it; but they do know they feel frustrated if their actions do not appear to "warrant" sex. They will feel resentful toward their partner for withholding what they feel they are owed, even if they would never use those words to describe the sense of injustice they feel. To trusted friends they may eventually explode and say something along the lines of: "I do x, y, and z around the house, I make sure everything is exactly how my partner wants it and still--nothing!" This exposes their true bias that sex is a system they are trying to game.

For the partner who sees sex as a system of punishment, sex is something they withhold to chasten their partner. If their partner has been slacking around the house or if they recently got into a fight, they might decide there's no sex this week--maybe no sex this month, depending on how slighted or frustrated they feel. They see sex as something they don't want but their partner does, and it makes logical sense to them that if their partner isn't sharing the burden of housework or childcare, or if they were rude and hurt their feelings, their behavior shouldn't be positively reinforced. Unconsciously they are conditioning their partner to associate sex with behavior, and this might be why their partner sees sex as a reward. But because this is a system of punishment, it won't actually help their partner to behave well...in the case of good behavior the absence of punishment serves as the reward. Of course, by doing nothing (as opposed to actively withholding), the outcome is the same: no sex. This system is both the carrot and the stick. It sets their partner up to fail no matter what.

In this paradigm the "punisher" is the more passive partner but ultimately has control. The "gamer" has a strategy that is doomed to fail because their helpful actions do not merit reward. And because both partners are operating within a system neither fully, consciously recognize, there is no way out. Both partners need to stop viewing sex as a transaction. This goes back to the damaging expectation of reciprocity--the tit-for-tat approach never works. The gamer should be helpful and kind to their partner with no expectation of reward. The punisher should base their decision to have sex solely on their own desire to--their partner's behavior may not stir their desire, but they should take responsibility for this response. They are not in charge of their partner's behavior, nor is it their job to discipline them. Because both partners are adults, both need to acknowledge their participation in this system and have the maturity to communicate their expectations, desires, and frustrations.

Just as there is a separation of church and state, sex and the everyday maintenance of a domestic life should be strictly divided. Sex should be as free from "real life" as possible--the best and healthiest sex is separated from who we are as husband and wife, mom and dad, son and daughter because the business of family has no place in sex. And sex should be a respite from our domestic duties. To transact sex as a reward or punishment for the nonsexual parts of our relationship is to banish the energy of eros and turn sex into a chore.

> *We cannot bargain the erotic in exchange for the unerotic without losing eroticism altogether.*

We are not "ourselves" per se, when we enjoy physical intimacy with our partner. Our sexual life with our partner allows us to experience a restorative break from the roles we perform in the commission of life's work. What we fantasize about and how we approach our lives, what we believe, and how we want to be treated. But paradoxically, we find great pleasure in the desires of our shadow selves and must be uninhibited by our "public-facing selves" in order to be free to explore them.

OUR PARTNER ISN'T THE ENEMY

THE 4 INTIMACY STYLES

PART III

THE KEY TO LASTING PHYSICAL INTIMACY

"Each Intimacy Style contains a hidden strength that benefits the whole of the sexual relationship."

- DR. VIVIANA

Chapter 7
The 4 Intimacy Styles Quiz ™

What Percentage Are You?
Take the digital version of this quiz and get your results calculated for you at www.4IntimacyStyles.com

Now that you know about each of the Intimacy Styles, you are ready to take the quiz and see what percentage of each you currently are: Bonding, Release, Giving, or Responsive.

NOTE: You will likely favor one Intimacy Style over the others, but the goal is to round out your intimate life by striving for 25% of each style in every sexual interaction.

Answer the following questions with the response that most matches what you would prefer in each scenario:

THE 4 INTIMACY STYLES

1. I FEEL MOST TURNED ON WHEN:

A. My partner and I are able to give and take in the bedroom and share in each other's pleasure.

B. I can just lie back and know that my partner will take care of me sexually.

C. I can explore and touch my partner's body and can tell that they are really turned on.

D. I don't usually know what's going to turn me on until it is happening.

2. I AM AT A SOCIAL EVENT AND SEE SOMEONE I AM ATTRACTED TO. I AM MOST LIKELY TO:

A. Walk over to the person and say, "Hi" and am thrilled when they smile and say, "Hi" back and ask me about myself.

B. Tap the person on the shoulder and introduce myself.

C. Make eye contact and wait for the person to approach me.

D. Stand near them and see what happens.

3. I AM READY FOR MY FIRST SEXUAL EXPERIENCE WITH MY PARTNER. I AM MOST LIKELY TO:

A. Enjoy taking charge and pulling them into the bedroom, but not until I know that they really like me and have shown interest in our relationship.

B. Show them with a long kiss and tight embrace.

C. Make subtle gestures to show I'm ready and hope that are too.

D. Stay quiet and wait to see if my partner will make a move when they are ready.

WHAT PERCENTAGE ARE YOU?

4. I WOULD HAVE TO END A RELATIONSHIP IF MY PARTNER:

A. Is always open to having sex but avoids sharing feelings about us after we have finished.

B. Avoids sexual activity altogether.

C. Always steers the conversation away from ever telling me what they prefer sexually.

D. Expects me to take the lead in most sexual activities and share my feelings about our sex life often.

5. I AM GOING OUT ON A DATE TO A MOVIE. I AM MOST LIKELY TO:

A. Initiate holding hands during the movie or be equally happy if they initiate holding hands first.

B. Initiate lots of playful touch during the movie.

C. Smile to myself every time my partner moves closer to me.

D. Hope my partner doesn't expect anything from me just like I don't expect anything from them.

6. WE WANT TO SPICE UP OUR SEX LIFE. I AM MOST LIKELY TO:

A. Feel hopeful that sharing both of our ideas will bring us closer together.

B. Buy that toy my partner mentioned they wanted to try with me and schedule a date to use it.

C. Listen for any clues as to what my partner would like to try and make sure to do those things.

D. Look up a new position to try in case they ever bring it up again.

THE 4 INTIMACY STYLES

A. Give a few sensual massages and be equally thrilled to have moments of sharing how compatible we are.
B. Look for any and all opportunities to get frisky with my partner.
C. Plan a bunch of special bedroom activities that I think my partner would love to do.
D. Go with the flow and not have any expectations.

A. Doesn't want me to initiate sexual activity and isn't interested in initiating either.
B. Is selfish in bed.
C. Doesn't like being the center of attention during sexual situations.
D. Nags me about sharing my fantasies.

A. Exchanging ideas with my partner about what we can do to feel even closer during sexual activity.
B. Giving my partner ideas of what I like and hearing my partner say they would like to do those things for me.
C. Listening to my partner express their fantasies and desires so that I know how to make the most out of our sexual relationship.
D. Listening to my partner express their feelings without any expectation for me to share.

10. MY PERFECT ROMANTIC PARTNER WOULD UNDERSTAND THIS ABOUT ME:

A. Having frequent physical affection in our relationship helps me to feel securely emotionally connected with them.

B. I love for my partner to pursue me and cater to my sexual needs.

C. It makes me feel good when I know I had something to do with my partner feeling good.

D. I am not really sexually-motivated and don't enjoy initiating sexual activities.

11. WHEN I HAVE A CRUSH ON SOMEONE, I AM MOST LIKELY TO:

A. Find excitement in fantasizing about how our sex life would be romantic and fulfilling forever.

B. Hope they show me signs that they are interested in me as well.

C. Find ways to show them that I'm interested that I think they'll respond well to.

D. Let my friends know I am interested and hope the information reaches my crush.

12. MY IDEAL SEXUAL EXPERIENCE INCLUDES:

A. "Making love" including giving and receiving pleasure with my partner.

B. Letting go of all control and receiving all the pleasure.

C. Taking charge and making sure my partner feels good.

D. Low-pressure activities that don't require a lot of effort but are satisfying to both of us.

THE 4 INTIMACY STYLES

13. FOR ME, "INTIMACY" MEANS:

A. Having an equal exchange of open communication and very few physical boundaries with my partner.

B. Showing my partner how sexually pleasing they are to me.

C. Showing my partner I care about them by being invested in their pleasure and feelings.

D. Connecting with my partner through shared experiences and quality time spent together.

14. A COZY NIGHT IN WITH MY PARTNER INCLUDES:

A. Trading off initiating fooling around on the couch while we binge watch a TV show.

B. Making sure that we spend most of the time aroused and sexually stimulated.

C. Ensuring that my partner is having a good time by planning out their favorite activities inside and outside the bedroom.

D. My partner would be content with just hanging out and enjoying sharing good conversation and cooking a nice meal together.

15. OUR DATE WENT WELL AND WE ARE SAYING GOODNIGHT. I AM MOST LIKELY TO:

A. Say that I really liked our time together and move in for a hug or a kiss.

B. Go straight in for a kiss.

C. Wait for any indication that they want to kiss, and then go in for one.

D. Just chill and see what happens.

WHAT PERCENTAGE ARE YOU?

Scoring

CHART OF PERCENTAGES FOR REFERENCE:

1 out of 15= 6.7%	6 out of 15= 40%	11 out of 15= 73.3%
2 out of 15= 13.3%	7 out of 15= 46.7%	12 out of 15= 80%
3 out of 15= 20%	8 out of 15= 53.3%	13 out of 15= 86.7%
4 out of 15= 26.7%	9 out of 15= 60%	14 out of 15= 93.3%
5 out of 15= 33.3%	10 out of 15= 66.7%	15 out of 15= 100%

_____ Percent As: BONDING Intimacy Style

Someone with a Bonding Intimacy Style enjoys physical intimacy because it helps them to feel emotionally bonded to their romantic partner. They seek out physical intimacy as a means to invest in a deeper level of connection in hopes of strengthening their level of commitment.

_____Percent Bs: RELEASE Intimacy Style

Someone with a Release Intimacy Style enjoys ensuring that they will experience a high level of physical pleasure during every sexual encounter. They seek out the rush and Release of physical tension from sexual pleasure and prioritize stimulation and orgasm.

_____ Percent Cs: GIVING Intimacy Style

Someone with a Giving Intimacy Style finds it more pleasurable to take a secondary role in sexual experiences. They derive contentment and sensual pleasure from Giving their partner sexual satisfaction.

_____ Percent Ds: RESPONSIVE Intimacy Style

Someone with a Responsive Intimacy Style is most comfortable with taking a more passive role and allowing their partner to take the lead in sexual activities. They prioritize sexuality when in response to their partner's needs.

Think about it:

Learning about your own Intimacy Style will benefit you enormously, but I also recommend reading about each Intimacy Style. You will gain a better understanding of your (potential) partner, and you'll also gain a new perspective. This perspective will help you integrate features of each Style into your own, allowing you to experience the full range of intimacy. It is my professional opinion that the healthiest Intimacy Style is a combination of all 4, amounting to 25% of each.

4

BONDING

THE 4 INTIMACY STYLES

Chapter 8
The BONDING Intimacy Style

Calling or texting throughout the day to check-in, sharing deeply personal stories, expressing physical affection, having lots of sex, being vulnerable...these are behaviors that show up in the cocoon of blissful, undisturbed early love. But for the person whose Intimacy Style is Bonding, this early process of merging with a partner never ends. They see life as a series of opportunities for spontaneity, emotional connection, and eroticism; they feel passion is a basic human right. They want to share all of this with their partner, the person they value most. Their partner is always their number one priority, often above their children, and certainly above any friendship or work obligation.

The bloom of a new relationship may be firmly affixed to the rose for them, but they will definitely feel nostalgic for the early days with their partner, simply because their partner shared their desire to deeply bond. In the beginning of a relationship, they bask in their partner's attunement. They revel in their partner's enthusiasm for sex. They may feel scared to be vulnerable to a new dating partner, but they also can't help themselves. The Bonding Style is the romantic of the Intimacy Styles; falling in love is easy for them, and they believe it can be forever--monogamy is a state they fantasize about and deeply enjoy once they achieve it.

Long after the relationship settles into a routine, bonding will continue to be their priority, and often the way they judge their success. If they're not secure in their primary relationship, it will cease to matter how satisfied they are at their job or in any other area, these achievements will feel hollow. Likewise, if their relationship is flourishing, they will feel as though their achievements and successes have meaning. It is the meaning they create in their relationship that drives them, and their purpose is their partner. They build their lives around them and feel that if their partner is happy, they are happy.

As their relationships go from casual to significant, this style is the type to crave commitment and actively seek it from their partner. A potential partner's ambivalence will feel threatening to them, and they will put thought and effort into establishing exclusivity. They're always looking for confirmation that they're safe, they're loved, and they're connected. They are devastated when their bids for connection are bypassed...and they feel shattered when they are explicitly rebuffed.

If they suffer too many of these slings and arrows (and it doesn't take much for this style), they will retreat into themselves for fear of rejection. They will become avoidant as a method of coping and hope their partner notices the shift. Unfortunately, the Bonding Style is often drawn to partners who have a very different Intimacy Style, a person who might not see anything wrong with the sudden distance, who might actually enjoy the arms' length of space. Their partner might feel relieved that the pace of early relationship sex and intense bonding has slowed down because to them, the profound intimacy the Bonding Style longs for can feel like a distraction, something they struggle to balance with the demands of daily life. Meanwhile, the Bonding Style struggles to feel balanced at all when they are not symbiotically connected to their partner.

When they feel rejected, the Bonding Style will find initiating sex intimidating, maybe even painful if their attempts are ever met with an excuse, an unenthused grunt, or an eye-roll. They may back off entirely and wait to see if their partner initiates instead. If their partner doesn't, and especially if this becomes the norm, the Bonding Style will come to regard their sex life as a dead bedroom. This is a state that will bring them daily despair and feelings of desperation. The longer it goes on, the more profoundly they will grieve. If they don't disclose to their partner how sad or desperate they're feeling, it's a guarantee that they are beyond a breaking point. I've seen it in my office many times: often the well-meaning but ignorant partner of a Bonding Style will express complete shock when they hear that their spouse is considering divorcing them over a lack of sex.

What these well-meaning partners need to understand is that it is never "just sex" in the Bonding Style of intimacy. To them, intimacy is a verb and sex is a powerful means of experiencing closeness. It's how they communicate their love, and it's how they gain reassurance and validation that their partner values them. They will have trouble understanding a partner who feels that sex is just an add-on, and not necessary to the success of the relationship. Or, even more unfathomable to them, a person that claims they could go without sex the rest of their life and be fine. The Bonding Style won't be able to conceive of it because relationships feel empty to them without sex, and their self-esteem suffers in its absence.

Sex makes the Bonding Style feel important. It affirms their existence in a way, as they feel fully seen, cared for, and beloved. When sex is off the table, they feel punished, and they will hunger for affirmation to displace the feeling that their partner takes them for granted. If the affirmation never comes, and especially if it's replaced by criticism, disregard, or shaming, they wilt like a dying plant. In the extreme, they become vulnerable to the slightest touch or compliment from strangers, coworkers, or friends. The smallest bit of attention will provide a shock of life-giving water and revive them, sometimes leading to an affair. When all is well for the Bonding Style, they wouldn't dream of cheating on their partner, but when their partner's affection cools, their identity becomes disorganized. They don't seek another for the physical release or thrill of the forbidden-- they long for a connection and to feel valued. They are looking for the fulfilled self they feel they have lost, rather than another person.

In lieu of an affair, they may disappear into other pursuits to try to offload the stress that builds up in their bodies, like working, exercising compulsively, or deadening their sensations by staring at a computer or phone screen for hours at a time. They will experience jealousy and despair watching other couples--the plots of romantic movies or tv shows will crush them, and they may not be able to tolerate watching a sex scene. The latter will inspire a seething rage and bitterness that they will probably not share with their partners. All will seem well on the outside or at least status quo, but inside the Bonding Style is in agony. Their sense of loss is acute.

So, what do you need if you're a Bonding Style, and what does the partner of a Bonding Style need to do to make you feel loved? The answer is not simply more sex. Often, the partners of a Bonding Style will see their desperation as a demand for more frequent sex and believe the need is purely physical. Sometimes this causes resentment in the other Intimacy Styles; they might even scoff and suggest that their partner's desires are perverse, and they should just "take care of themselves." Imagine a record scratch loudly disrupting this paragraph so I can warn you: there is almost nothing more hurtful you could say to a Bonding Style than that. They will feel exiled from the relationship and objectified as if they're a car in need of an oil change instead of a human being longing to connect. While they do indeed crave the physical satisfaction of more frequent sex, as well as the high of oxytocin and dopamine, the idea that they're only seeking an orgasm is offensive to them because to them, the act is meaningless if their partner is reluctant.

The Bonding Style does not want to experience "pity sex," "duty sex," or "homework sex." In other words, if you're having sex with them because you pity them for feeling rejected, or because you feel obligated as part of a bargain with them, or because a sex therapist or self-help book "assigned" sex, you may as well ditch sex entirely for all the good it's doing them. No matter how well you try to hide your motivations, a Bonding Style will always be able to pick up on them--they are hypersensitive and emotionally perceptive individuals who scan their partners for nonverbal cues. If they sense their partner withdrawing or feel that their partner isn't enjoying sex with them, the Bonding Style is very likely to take it personally and may even go so far as to feel ashamed and disgusted with themselves. Their motto is:

"I want you to want me."

What's important to this Intimacy Style is feeling wanted and anything less will only frustrate them more. A lot of couples struggling to reignite a passion for each other believe the adage that sex begets more sex, and many sex therapists will use the refrain "Just do it!" as a method of reviving a stagnant sex life. In some contexts and within certain relationships, this is a good idea. Scheduling weekly sex, as unsexy and unspontaneous as that prospect may seem, can create the space necessary for a busy couple to engage in a meaningful connection. There is something about purposely setting aside a few hours that makes the time seem more valuable, and the act more special. However, this simple method may be too simple for a Bonding Style, as it doesn't address the *wanting* they crave from their partners. Scheduling an appointment doesn't necessarily mean you want to go through with it, and to the Bonding Style, the scheduling itself will strike them as cold; a way to automate something they feel should come naturally. They feel that way because intimacy comes naturally to *them*.

CASE STUDY:

Meet Brenden

Brenden came to see me because he was struggling to feel physically and mentally aroused during sex with his most recent partners. With pleading, earnest eyes, he explained that he had trouble experiencing sexual pleasure when he sleeps with someone he doesn't feel close to. He doesn't feel right about having sex with someone unless he feels that they "click." I could tell that he had probably tried to share this with previous partners and was met with a mocking, incredulous look. After all, our society assumes "men only want one thing." He went on to share that he has, at times, fooled around with someone he just met but immediately regretted it and vowed not to do it again. Exasperated, he said, "It just isn't worth it, and I feel like my body agrees with me. But it's hard to date and wait to have sex until I feel close enough to someone. No one seems to have time for that these days."

He's not wrong. So many of the singles I work with have shared that there is a widely-held belief that sex is expected to happen by the third in-person date. That kind of pressure creates anxiety around dating, even digital dating. After so many digital interactions, an in-person meeting is expected to become an opportunity to sexually get to know each other. For someone like Brenden, these expectations can wreak havoc on his sexual functioning way before climbing into bed with someone. Brenden wants to feel close, connected, and comfortable with a partner to really enjoy sex.

Brenden wistfully shared with me that the best sex of his life happened the night he proposed to his ex. There was something so comforting about knowing that they had just committed to being each other's partner in all ways including sexually, forever. They ended their engagement 7 months later and for the past 10 months, he hasn't had a fulfilling sexual experience with anyone. Clearly distraught, Brenden openly admitted to being frustrated with himself and with his body. He wanted to know why he can't just "enjoy sex like everyone else does: with no strings attached."

Brenden's Intimacy Style is Bonding. When he engages in any sexual activity with a partner, his main motivation is to leave that interaction feeling emotionally closer to them and vice versa. In sharing his physical body and showing a desire to experience shared pleasure with his partner, he feels bonded to them. But, if Brenden continues to solely desire to bond during sexual experiences, he will miss out on the other relationship benefits of sex with future partners I have laid out in this book.

The key to rounding out his intimate connection with any future partner/s would be to put effort into experiencing all four of the Intimacy Styles in each sexual interaction. For Brenden, the Bonding Style comes naturally to him, so we focused on Release, Giving, and Responsive Styles. For Release, I asked him to name the most physically pleasurable sexual activity to him and tell me why and instructed him to incorporate it into his next sexual experience. For Giving, I asked him to recall a time when his ex had shared being very pleased with a sexual experience and asked him to consider trying to introduce it into his next sexual experience. For Responsive, other than the aforementioned recommendations, I asked him to sit back and allow his new partner to take the lead so as to reduce his sexual anxiety.

Like so many others who are committed to the work they do with me, Brenden pushed through his own discomfort and came to realize that by "rounding out" his Intimacy Style, he could enjoy sexual interactions with more frequency and with more confidence. This has allowed him to get further than he had with dating to find a partner.

FOR THE PARTNERS OF THOSE WITH A BONDING INTIMACY STYLE:

You were chosen, carefully and deliberately, by the Bonding Style you're in a relationship with. They don't want sex for the sake of it, they want sex with _you_, to feel closer to _you_. Be assured that even if they no longer initiate sex, their need for intimacy hasn't gone away. They have simply done their best to bury it underground in an attempt to accommodate you and protect themselves. What goes unsaid is likely a major source of stress for them and tension between you. The best support you can give them is to take their intimacy needs seriously. Listen to them without judgment. Then show them it matters to you by exploring why you feel sexually inhibited. What is preventing you from enjoying intimacy with your partner?

Just seeing you proactively address the issue will do wonders for their self-esteem. And exploring mental and physical blocks to intimacy with a qualified therapist can help you with _your_ self-esteem, which will also help your partner. They need you to hold up a sex-positive mirror that reflects acceptance and a fully inhabited sexuality.

Be aware that a Bonding Style will accept other forms of physical affection without transitioning to sex, but you need to explicitly set that boundary. If they don't know what direction you're headed, they might anticipate sex and be disappointed when you break away. Understanding your partner's sensitivity in this regard will help you to experience touch at your level of comfort without anxiety and save them the agony of feeling unwanted. But I also recommend you prioritize a couple of sexual interactions with your partner each week in whatever environment feels safest to you and allow yourself to truly sync up with your partner--try to focus on the intimacy you're building together.

Above all, communicate everything you've avoided talking about. Without communication, the Bonding Style assumes their partner doesn't care. Tell your partner what's holding you back, how you feel about it, and what you plan to do about it. Express a willingness to work on your intimacy with each other. Simply saying these things might reduce your partner's resentment by half. That said, in the words of Deepak Chopra, "Love without action is meaningless, and action without love is irrelevant." It will be important to follow through on your plans to integrate your intimacy needs with theirs, especially if your Bonding Style partner has experienced feelings of abandonment in the relationship.

To review, what's important to remember about the Bonding Style is that they are the intimacy experts: they welcome it, they cultivate it, and they need it. The strength of their craving for closeness cannot be underestimated or undervalued. To them, closeness is non-negotiable; they will consider ending the relationship over its lack, regardless of how otherwise functional the relationship is. They might love their partner very much, feel they and their partner are effective as a team, get along great, and have a mutually satisfying friendship with each other, but the glaring lack of a physically intimate life might tip the scales for them. They might also, over time, try to hide their needs to avoid being hurt by their partner's indifference, resulting in bitterness and resentment. They may initiate less or not at all, but the unmet need never goes away.

The partner of a Bonding Style should not see their need as an impatient demand for sex, rather, they should consider it their partner's deep desire for significance--a longing to be seen, held, and cherished. They should avoid belittling their partner's need by suggesting it's perverse or purely physical; they should certainly avoid banishing them to masturbation, as "taking care of themselves" will never achieve their primary and eternal goal of bonding.

BONDING

Think about it:

Learning about your own Intimacy Style will benefit you enormously, but I also recommend reading about each Intimacy Style. You will gain a better understanding of your (potential) partner, and you'll also gain a new perspective. This perspective will help you integrate features of each Style into your own, allowing you to experience the full range of intimacy. It is my professional opinion that the healthiest Intimacy Style is a combination of all 4, amounting to 25% of each.

THE 4 INTIMACY STYLES

Chapter 9
The RELEASE Intimacy Style

Understanding intimacy as sexual release may strike some in our culture as a contradiction in terms. While we obsess over the mechanics and complications of the male orgasm through a clinical lens or devote social analysis to the prevarication of the female orgasm, we tend to see sexual climax in either gender as strictly physical. We mythologize the obscurity of the clitoris, treating its potential for orgasm as an intractable puzzle to solve, while the solution to troublesome male orgasm comes in pill form, its prescribed users tripling in recent years. We are a society that focuses on outcomes and we'll go to great lengths to get results, while the hard work of intimacy--nonlinear and non-measurable as it is, is not something we associate with the unmistakable success of sexual climax.

Release as an Intimacy Style can indeed be understood as an investment in the denouement of sex, particularly the potent hormonal charge that accompanies it. Oxytocin, also known as "The Love Drug," floods the brain upon orgasm, creating a feeling of bliss and prompting couples to remain in physical contact during the soothing, hazy afterglow. For the Release Style, the experience of erupting pleasure followed by deep relaxation as the oxytocin flows is the ideal vehicle for intimacy. Oxytocin is also the hormone mothers produce after giving birth and while they breastfeed, which allows them to bond with their infants, compelling behaviors like gazing and cuddling--which are not too far from the behavior it promotes in post-coital couples. Someone whose Intimacy Style is Release is especially sensitive to these effects. They associate the pleasant and relaxing high with their love for their partner and attribute the euphoria of orgasm to their partner's efforts. Their partner is their hero at this moment, and admiration and gratitude will rise to the level of their heart rate.

Far from having a singular focus on outcome, the Release Style seeks within climax a warmth and connection. But their ardent pursuit can sometimes leave a bad impression. They are indeed driven by their urges and they *are* chasing a high, which their partner can misinterpret as mindless carnal lust, something they might feel for anyone with a pulse. But the Release Style is not indiscriminate. It is more accurate to say that experiencing orgasm with their partner brings their feelings of love and devotion into sharp focus, whereas those feelings might dull or be inaccessible to them after a period of lowered sexual engagement. Oxytocin is released with each sexual interaction, and while the Release Style enjoys any activity that leads to oxytocin production, reaching orgasm with a partner is their favorite way to maintain a steady level of it. That means they enjoy high frequency sexual interactions. Unlike the Bonding Style, whose fantasies of romance, monogamy, and specialness drive their desire to physically connect, the Release Style will crave physical connection as a way to infuse their relationship with meaning. If a feeling of emotional intimacy leading to physical intimacy could be understood as a top-down approach, the Release Style is bottom-up:

Physical intimacy opens the door to emotional intimacy.

The Release Style enjoys quickies as well as long drawn-out sessions that ideally include more than one round of sex. But in either scenario, they enter a trance-like state that feels as raw and animalistic as it does mystical and disembodied. Sex is an act of meditation for them, in which they direct an energy of consummation toward their partner. If you could look inside the brain of a Release Style during sex, you would surely see that sexual pleasure lights up their reward pathways, with the accompanying surge of dopamine flowing freely. Dopamine is known to create emotional associations during and after orgasm as a feeling of complete contentment and satisfaction washes over them, their desire for their partner is reinforced. This is the style that can't get enough of your love.

With the unleashing of dopamine and oxytocin comes another reward for the Release Style: confidence. They exit the act with a bit of swagger. They feel sexy, attractive, and appreciated, and this heightened and favorable view of themselves will act as yet another motivator to pursue sex again. The Release Style experiences a vitality from sex that makes them feel younger and healthier, as well as a feeling of peace that confirms all is right with the world. They feel loved and supported by their partner which banishes any feelings of isolation or depression they might otherwise experience.

The Release Style enjoys the anticipation of sex and enjoys mental as well as physical foreplay. Sexting and sexual touch without immediately transitioning to sex are incredibly stimulating to them and make them much more focused on their partner and their relationship. The Release Style sees a long-term relationship as a lifetime of dating their partner. They will put effort into planning little retreats and activities for just the two of them, and usually consider long sessions of physical intimacy part of the itinerary.

In fact, any activity with the Release Style can feel erotic; they enjoy the intimacy of activities that require preparation and time together, like cooking and savoring a meal. They enjoy sharing with their partner, even something as simple as sharing a bucket of popcorn at the movie theatre or sharing a blanket to snuggle together on the couch. The Release Style will probably enjoy the intimacy of going clothes shopping together and helping each other pick outfits. Then, anytime their partner wears an item they picked out for them, they'll feel a buzz of pleasure.

The Release Style also enjoys novelty. Going to new places with their partner or doing things they never have before will give them an erotic charge. They love bonding with their partner over a new experience. They're also very open to new sexual techniques or positions and tend to be enthusiastically supportive of their partner's curiosity and interests. That said, they are also respectful of their partner's boundaries because they want sex to be as stress-free as possible.

The Release Style feels the most validated when their partner prioritizes their pleasure. Partners who don't place much importance on orgasm or don't see it as "the point" of sex will frustrate the Release Style, who doesn't feel sex is complete unless both partners experience the most pleasure possible. Partners who don't feel they need to orgasm to enjoy sex will utterly confound them. But they can manage a successful relationship with them, as long as sex doesn't dry up completely.

Just as with the Bonding Style, the Release Style feels rejected when sex is denied, and will also suffer withdrawal symptoms. These will manifest slightly differently and can be much more intense. They're quite literally addicted to this form of intimacy and might become sour without it. Of all the styles, they suffer the most from a discrepancy of desire with their partner and will likely raise the issue frequently and perhaps even criticize their partner. In response, their partner may come to see them as needy and deflect their advances with their own criticism.

In the absence of regular sex with their partner, they usually resign themselves to daily masturbation which will be unsatisfying to them since they're really after closeness. As such, in moments of desperation some will consider finding an affair partner. But because physical release is the way they access feelings of intimacy, this idea will lack appeal. They want this experience with their partner. They want it so much they will feel distracted going through life, unable to focus on tasks. They will feel stuck at this point, unable to entice their partner into sex, and left without any other options. Like the Bonding style, they will eventually bury their feelings and experience resentment.

Just as with the Bonding style's hiding, a Release Style who stops fighting for intimacy is on the brink of collapse. They will probably feel a wave of simmering anger just underneath a stoic exterior that they don't share with their partner. They might ask their partner to attend couples counseling or to see a sex therapist with them but if their partner demurs or doesn't do the work in therapy, they will consider dissolving the relationship as their next option. Meanwhile, their partner may not even be aware of the Release Style's anguish. Or, if they become aware, they might not take their feelings seriously, which will ultimately do the most harm.

Of all the Intimacy Styles, the Release Style may encounter the most conflict with the Responsive Style. It's not that these two can't be compatible because they absolutely can; the Release Style is happy to initiate, and the Responsive style finds them less ambiguous than other Styles which makes it easier to follow their lead. But if these two get stuck in a pattern of initiation and rejection, they will have considerable difficulty getting themselves un-stuck. These two might want to look into unconscious logic or consider pursuer-distancer dynamics or the system of punishment versus reward in earlier chapters.

The Release Style is apt to fall back on childhood scripts with the Responsive Style, and generally these intersect the childhood experiences of both partners in a perfect cross-section of learned behaviors. And by "perfect," I mean each partner plays a role representative of an early relationship in the other's life, and these roles dredge up their respective unresolved attachment issues. These issues seem tailor-made to recreate the dysfunction each experienced. Because sex and childhood experience don't mix (to say nothing of familial roles), this pattern effectively terminates the erotic energy between them.

Whether the Release Style gets rejected by the Responsive Style or by the other Intimacy Styles is less important than the unsafe feeling they experience in the absence of regular sex. The Release Style depends on sex to provide mental and emotional balance. The chemical high of sex affects the Release Style the way an antidepressant or exercise might work for someone else. They seek sex not only for the buzz they feel when they're connected to their partner, but the stress relief it provides. Without it, they may indeed turn to antidepressants or exercise but neither establishes intimacy in their partnership, which in turn stresses them out. Being shut out by their partner makes them feel as if they're experiencing this conflict alone, or that they're on the outside of their relationship looking in. They ultimately won't feel emotionally safe.

If the Release Style does have regular sex with a partner, they experience the benefits of lowered stress like better mood, better sleep, and better self-regulation. They're more invested in their relationship and spend more time with their partner. The world has more color, and they have a resilience they don't otherwise possess. Sex looks good on them, in other words. They thrive in a relationship that is sex-positive and with a partner who doesn't express disgust or assign shame to their intimate life together. And they're in heaven with a partner who understands and doesn't diminish their fundamental need for release.

CASE STUDY:
Meet Raquel

Raquel came to see me because she was feeling guilty after being told by a friend that she should seek professional advice about never having experienced an emotional connection to a sexual partner. She seemed self-conscious as she said she hadn't ever realized that she hadn't ever "made love" to anyone and just figured it was a myth in rom-coms and Harlequin novels. She had been told she was "like a guy" when it comes to sex over drinks and laughs with friends. She never took it to heart or minded until her last relationship ended, and the same phrase was thrown at her with pain and hurt and tears in their eyes. She vowed to figure out if there was something more that she hadn't experienced or was incapable of experiencing.

Raquel is a Release Style who sees sex as her form of stress relief. She loves the way her mind clears and her body tension disappears after an orgasm. She enjoys the physicality of it all: the sweat, the smells, the stretching, the messiness. She feels like she can rule the world after she has sex and experiences a "runner's high" after doing the deed. She thoroughly enjoyed the thrill of the chase and was proud to have never experienced a "Walk of Shame." Afterall, she is a modern woman who doesn't need to feel ashamed of seeking sexual satisfaction.

The best sex of her life was on an 8-day trip to Fiji with 3 of her best friends. She says she met a local guy and they spent most of the trip trying every sex position imaginable and felt free to do whatever she needed to do to reach orgasm. She recalls laughing about staying hydrated and being sore for about a week after.

Raquel came to see me because her last two significant others broke up with her over this. They said they felt like she was using them for sex and "didn't have a romantic bone in her body." Raquel wants to make sure that her next relationship won't end because her partner believes she is incapable of experiencing any emotional connection during sex.

Raquel's Intimacy Style is Release. When she is engaging in any sexual activity with a partner, she is hoping that it will allow her to experience a rush of pleasure and to release physical tension through orgasm. She feels empowered and proud to have a body that can experience peak pleasure. She feels badly for anyone who has had "bad sex" because there is no way she would ever let that happen to her. She pities her friends in monotonous, predictable sexual relationships. In so many ways, Raquel is lucky. But, if Raquel continues to solely desire to orgasm during sexual experiences, she will miss out on the other relationship benefits of sex with future partners.

The key to rounding out her intimate connection with any future partner/s would be to put effort into experiencing all four of the Intimacy Styles into each sexual experience. For Raquel, the Release Style comes naturally to her, so we focused on Bonding, Giving, and Responsive Styles. For Bonding, I asked Raquel to consider when she has cared for a close friend or relative and how she felt when she was able to be helpful to them in their time of need. What fond feelings did she imagine they felt toward her? For Giving, I asked her to consider what it would possibly feel like if even when she was trying to make sure her own needs were met, she had a partner who didn't comply or care enough to stick around long enough to make sure that she was able to get there. For Responsive, I asked Raquel to, upon her next sexual experience, not begin and end with her own orgasmic pursuit. What would it look like if she took a backseat and let her partner's pleasure take the wheel?

Like so many others who are committed to the work they do with me, Raquel consistently chose sexual altruism and came to realize that by "rounding out" her Intimacy Style, she could enjoy sexual interactions with more frequency and with more confidence. This has given her the opportunity to be a more attractive sexual partner and has promoted her wish to find a long-term partner.

FOR THE PARTNERS OF THOSE WITH A RELEASE INTIMACY STYLE:

Your partner finds it easiest to connect with you through sex and after sex. This is not because they view you as a sex object, it is because they feel the most loved after experiencing physical closeness with you. They also feel the most confident about expressing love through physical intimacy--they can certainly be a supportive and emotionally available partner, but sex is the language they're fluent in.

It will be unclear, even to themselves, if sex drives them to connect or if the connection they have with you drives them to want sex because sex and connection exist in an endless feedback loop for them. Without sex they feel disconnected and frankly lost, but without an intimate connection, they're unenthused about sex. They're not so desperate that they'll take sex anywhere, in any form because, as with the Bonding Style, a reluctant partner is a turn-off. And because sex and intimate emotional connection are so entwined for them, that turn-off will extend to the entire relationship.

Partnered sex is an occasion for them. They look forward to it and they plan it out in their minds. If sex were a dinner party, they would be the consummate host laboring over every detail. For that matter, they're also the guest, as they take great pleasure in consuming what is offered and feel flattered by the special attention they receive from you. Sex with a partner who is not attentive to them is sex that falls flat. They also appreciate enthusiasm. Partners who want to "just get it over with" or complain that sex isn't "everything" in a relationship will wound the Release Style, who often feels insecure about their love of sex. Generally, they've experienced this shame in some form in their lives, either from family or former partners.

They feed off of the intimacy you co-create in the pleasure you share as a couple. They want you to be in the same space as them, feeling what they feel. They love the feeling of merging as they become physically part of you. They want to revisit this space again and again--it never gets tiresome for them, and even though they like novelty, they're rarely bored by the sexual routines you establish as a couple. They like knowing what works for them and what works for you.

Sometimes the partner of a Release Style knows intuitively that the more sex they have, the more they want it, and feels reluctant to start on this cycle. In this case, communication about how to meet both your needs is important. The Release Style is perfectly capable of compromising, they just need to know where the boundaries are. They're also game to adapt to and integrate their partner's Intimacy Style. As long as sex isn't off the table completely, they're happy to experiment with frequency and quality of sexual interaction to reach a sweet spot that meets both partners' needs.

In a way, the Release Style sees sex and the subsequent high of orgasm as a short cut to bond with you. They may not consciously realize they feel anxious or need reassurance but often they seek to soothe attachment anxiety through sex. They also find sex, as well as time together leading up to sex, to be the best and most impactful way to express their love for you. If they feel there's been distance between you, sex is their way of reuniting. Sex inherently contains all the passion, the closeness, and the intensity of their feelings, so it says the words they can't always find. Sex is the route they travel, but intimacy is the destination.

If your Release Style partner seems withdrawn, or isn't initiating sex, you can be sure they're feeling unmoored, angry, abandoned, and anxious. Sex gives them endorphins and energy, and when they're not having any, their mental health suffers. To some extent, any focused, intimate time together will help to offset their melancholy, but they will also feel any activity with you is incomplete if sex--even just sexual teasing or flirting--isn't a part of it. Their physical longing for it can be compared to a deep, gnawing hunger. And just like hunger doesn't go away unless you eat, the Release Style won't be satiated unless they have sex--and then it's only a matter of time before they're ravenous again. Just like the Bonding Style doesn't get much benefit from masturbation, and in fact feels it's a banishment from the relationship, the Release Style will deeply resent feeling they have to masturbate to quell their urges. They may spend hours in a despondent mental spiral, lying awake next to you as you slumber unaware. It's not too much to say the Release Style experiences grief when they're repeatedly denied sexual intimacy.

They won't know how to close the gap that exists between you, and probably fear you don't want to. They probably feel taken for granted and cast aside. They might also feel trapped and stagnant; unable to abandon their needs, but unable to get them met. They know that it's wrong to cajole a partner into sex, and they will feel too humiliated to beg. Without any options they experience frustration, desperation, and despair. They will most certainly long for emotional connection and they might feel isolated even when they're in the same room as you.

Making an effort to understand and respect their Intimacy Style and their feelings will put the Release Style at ease, who worries that their partner doesn't care about their needs, or that their partner is disgusted by them. Scheduling "check-ins" with each other, as well as times to have sexual intimacy, will assure the Release Style that you are prioritizing them and that you value the relationship. Making every effort to resolve desire discrepancy will validate the Release Style and will also improve their patience. They sincerely don't want to overwhelm their partner with demands. In fact, they don't want to have to demand sex at all, but they also can't handle long periods of sexlessness without experiencing depression. As their partner, it's important to manage their expectations and help their confidence by specifying your intentions. The not knowing is the worst part for the Release Style who believes they've been sexually abandoned when their partner doesn't address their different intimacy needs.

———————— *Think about it:* ————————

Learning about your own Intimacy Style will benefit you enormously, but I also recommend reading about each Intimacy Style. You will gain a better understanding of your (potential) partner, and you'll also gain a new perspective. This perspective will help you integrate features of each Style into your own, allowing you to experience the full range of intimacy. It is my professional opinion that the healthiest Intimacy Style is a combination of all 4, amounting to 25% of each.

THE 4 INTIMACY STYLES

Chapter 10
The GIVING Intimacy Style

Many people disappear into the act of sex as if masked at a costume ball. They don characteristics and preferences that contradict their day-to-day selves and together with their partner explore an inversion of reality. But for those who identify as the Giving Style of intimacy, sex is a reflection of who they are in their relationship. They are the consummate giver; they give their all in their jobs, they give their energy and a listening ear to their family and friends, they give their praise and support to their partners, and they give help wherever it is needed. They often have an easygoing temperament and genuinely enjoy being in service to others, especially their partner. They're not competitive or overly ambitious. They're not combative or easily flustered. They don't mind doing grunt work. If there's only one slice of cake left, they much prefer giving it to their partner overeating it themselves.

They experience intimacy as a journey and pleasure as a process, and settle in to sex with their partner like a maestro conducting an orchestra. They use as many sensual "instruments" to bring pleasure as there are body parts--they use their voice, hands, even their gaze to build their partner's anticipation. Attentive to every squirm and moan, they're apt to find erogenous zones their partner wasn't even aware of. They love the way their partner looks in the throes of pleasure and do their level best to make them lose all conscious awareness of themselves and their surroundings. While other styles see orgasm as the main event or the finale, the Giving Style tends to see it as the opening act. They will typically bring a partner to climax more than once, usually before even considering intercourse. It's not hard to see that the Giving Style is considered by most to be an incomparable lover; their partners often credit them as the best sex they've ever had.

The Giving Style is genuinely more turned on by their partner's arousal than anything their partner could do for them. They seem to experience pleasure vicariously, and almost voyeuristically. They don't need their partner's touch; in fact, they prefer the titillation of watching their partner's euphoric expressions and frenzied movement. They feel as if they could spend hours giving their partner pleasure and they often do. It's not uncommon for them to use the phrase:

"I could do this all day."

They love the challenge of learning a new partner's rhythms and desires and finding all their most sensitive places. They consider themselves lifelong students of the art of intimacy. Their long-term partners realize how lucky they are and they're often the envy of close friends.

Despite their partners' enthusiasm, the Giving Style might be bewildered by a paradox in their long-term relationships; given enough time, their partners might start to feel frustrated with the intense one-sided focus on their pleasure. They will want very much to give something back and will feel defeated when they try. It's not that the Giving Style never accepts pleasure, but their partners will often want to return the lengthy and extremely focused attention *they* get, and this proposition can get uncomfortable for the Giving Style. It's difficult for them to understand that their partner is also turned on by giving pleasure because the Giving Style decided early that most people had sex for their own pleasure, and that honing in on their partner would give them an edge and make them unique. The Giving Style feels anxious and guilty if their partner goes to any lengths to please them (and they also worry that they're losing their specialness if they take instead of receive). They might even try to cut their partner's attempts short to return attention to them. This will only frustrate their partner more, who might feel they're always in the Giving Style's debt. Their partner might also complain about a lack of intimacy, as non-reciprocal sex can sometimes feel disconnected from emotion. The Giving Style's dissociation from their own arousal might make their partner feel they are not really "there." It might seem like the Giving Style is in a trance, fixated solely on creating pleasure for pleasure's sake. This can almost seem mechanical, as if their partner's body is a circuit board and they're wiring connections and flipping switches.

The essence of this behavior extends outside the bedroom. The Giving Style often lets go of things they want and feels uncomfortable if a partner tries to provide them because deep down, they're afraid of disappointing or upsetting others. They may have learned early on in life that if they set aside their own needs and desires, they could avoid conflict or abandonment. Because they've so deeply internalized a belief that if they're not the ones giving, they're unlovable and cause resentment, they can't allow their partner to do much for them. And they fear that if they were to give too little, they would be rejected.

The Giving Style is also vulnerable to toxic relationships. They are at risk of finding partners who primarily take in relationships, and who end up exploiting the Giving Style's indulgence. These partners may become lazy and unhealthily dependent on the generosity of the Giving Style, and allow themselves to be cared for almost like a child. Because the Giving Style's capacity to give is like a bottomless well, these types of partners can take advantage of them for years before the Giving Style experiences burn out. But the Giving Style is also aware of this dynamic and aware of their good nature, so they have difficulty accepting any criticism. Giving is their strategy to avoid conflict, after all. When it doesn't work, the Giving Style builds resentment and even rage against their partner; they seem to believe that their endless caretaking should guarantee they're never in trouble.

In this way they are relying on an implied contract that says they will prioritize their partner's happiness and sweep their shortcomings under the rug while their partner agrees never to have complaints. While it's true that this kind of relationship is unbalanced and unfair for them, it's important for a Giving Style to see how they're contributing to this dilemma. They need to form a boundary between themselves and their partner in order to recognize that their needs are a priority too, and they can't expect someone else to meet them by denying they exist.

They are also not responsible for meeting *all* their partner's needs. They need to accept that it's ok for their partner to meet their own needs and to be upset with them--that this doesn't negate their good traits. The Giving Style needs to realize it's possible to accept they're not always the perfect partner and still maintain their self-worth. Healthy boundaries include taking accountability without taking on shame.

That said, an exploitive partner may intuitively know the Giving Style's weak spots and may use shame as an incentive to get even *more* out of the Giving Style. The Giving Style finds contempt or criticism unbearable and if their partner subjects them to either, they will redouble their efforts, hoping to guarantee they won't be targeted going forward. This usually turns into a cycle of submitting and trying harder every time their partner gets angry. Eventually they will feel overwhelmed--they don't know how to manage conflict when giving doesn't work.

There is nothing inherently flawed about the Giving Style of intimacy--quite the opposite. They are naturally skilled at intimacy, they just need to realize they have worth outside of caring and providing for others and protect their own needs with boundaries. They will find it relatively easy to integrate their style with any of the other 3 Intimacy Styles--their style is compatible with the goals of Bonding and Release and they're happy to provide the context and motivation necessary to captivate a Responsive Style. With each individual style, the Giving Style's challenge will be to allow their partner to occasionally take charge in the bedroom to give *them* pleasure, but also to make sure they don't allow their partner to take charge of the entire relationship. They need to prioritize their own emotional needs alongside their partner's.

For the Giving Style to evolve to their full potential, it will be important to shift their relationship paradigm to a more holistic view of what makes a relationship successful. The Giving Style's internalized belief that the absence of conflict guarantees their safety includes the belief that zero conflict equals success. They feel if their partner is unhappy, or if they ever fight with their partner, that they have failed and the relationship is under threat. As a result, they struggle with vulnerability, the main ingredient of intimacy. If they don't feel safe every time their partner has a bad day, and if they feel they can't reveal their own negative thoughts and feelings lest they risk the relationship, their relationships will always suffer from disconnection and low intimacy. By doing what they think will save their partner and the relationship, they're actually ensuring the opposite.

They might believe their abundant generosity and good heart are all that's needed to find harmony with a partner, and our culture reinforces this idea. We uphold a romantic myth of the "good man," or "good woman," who demonstrates chivalry and/or undying loyalty. What's ironic, and often devastating to a Giving Style, is that these same qualities that start off as so attractive are often the very qualities that create an unhealthy relationship dynamic and can even cause resentment in their partners. Loyalty taken to the extreme requires an abandonment of self, particularly if one finds themselves at odds with the partner they've sworn loyalty to. When the Giving Style buries their needs and feelings to prop up an idealized image of themself and preserve the relationship at great cost to their own needs, their partner can sense it. When they are unceasingly chivalrous, they can become so focused on protecting their partner that they disrespect their own needs as well as their partner's ability to solve their own problems. And ultimately, these self-sacrificial acts make their partner feel unsafe.

The partner of a Giving Style who takes advantage of their giving nature and domineers them with criticism is one who feels insecure in the relationship. They're issuing a challenge based on their feelings of unsafety. If you could translate their hostile attacks with closed captioning, their subtitles would read:

Hey! I know I'm not supposed to have this much power in a relationship. I know you're not telling me what's bothering you in order to accommodate me. This makes me worry about what else you might be hiding. Can I trust you? And while we're on the subject, I don't feel worthy of your generosity and your care. Look at me tearing you apart right now! Someone like me doesn't deserve someone like you. Please make my self-concept make sense and agree with me or take me out of this misery and convince me I'm wrong.

People with childhood experiences of abandonment (and we have all had these experiences to an extent, since our parents were only human and could not be immediately available to us 24/7, nor could they always be available in the specific ways we needed them to be) will choose defense mechanisms in order to cope, and often people who end up in relationships together have chosen opposite methods of coping. One might cope by denying their own needs and trying to be as unburdensome as possible; another might choose to start arguments because negative attention is better than no attention; another might decide that abandoning others before they get the chance to abandon them is the best way to avoid loss and shame. The

Giving Style's method of coping is to deny their own needs and instead focus exclusively and quite intensely on their partner's needs. They come to their rescue, they praise and flatter them, they indulge them, they pamper them--and all of this is an elaborate means to avoid an end. When the Giving Style finds themselves being criticized and threatened with abandonment *anyway*, the solution is *not* to frantically redouble their efforts. Trying harder and giving more will not work. The solution is to finally risk vulnerability and share their fears with their partner.

As I mentioned above, the critical or demanding partner of the Giving Style is acting on their own abandonment fears. They understand the Giving Style is sacrificing their own needs, and they know this is wrong. They question their worth in the relationship because they've become overly dependent on the Giving Style and underfunctioning as a result. Knowing this about their partner offers the Giving Style a clue to how they should approach a conversation with them. It will help to project confidence in this discussion because their partner needs safety and reassurance just as much as they do. Both partners need to consider boundaries, but the Giving Style should lead the charge here. They have conditioned their partner to take, and takers don't set limits, so they have to.

After an acknowledgement of both partners' fears of abandonment, the Giving Style should steer this conversation to include a disclosure of their own wants and needs. Giving voice to these will prove powerful. The Giving Style should go further by asking their partner to meet an emotional and a sexual need of theirs.

If the Giving Style continues having difficulty allowing their partner to focus on them in the bedroom, it might be helpful for them to take a break from sex for several weeks to reconnect with themselves. During this moratorium, they should do anything they find personal gratification in and focus on their enjoyment. If thoughts of others or worries about self-indulgence appear they should just observe them as they occur and let them fade.

During this period of time, they can try any activity other than sex that gives them physical, sensual pleasure...anything from walking barefoot in the sand, to relaxing in a hammock, to taking a nice, warm bath. They should stay grounded in these moments as much as possible, focusing on their body's sensations. The point of these exercises is to experience receiving pleasure without feeling any concern about a partner. When they do reintroduce sexual activity, they can call on these experiences to remind themselves to surrender to the pleasure their partner offers them. They can also try my version of sensate focus (The Dr. Viviana Method for Intimate Reconnection©) as a way to reintroduce sex. The rules governing time for giving and receiving make sure partners are touched and do the touching equally.

Above all, it is important for the Giving Style to know that being "taken by" (rather than given to) is a turn-on. It can feel very liberating when our sexual partner is consumed by their own lust and seeks their own pleasure in us. Sometimes, to be catered to produces a feeling similar to that of being taken care of, and associating caretaking with sex will always blunt erotic urges. Two adults acting on their passion for each other does not borrow from feelings involved in obligation or self-sacrifice. It is precisely the selfish nature of sexual indulgence that divorces sex from duty. Of course, it is important to be mindful of our partner's pleasure and attend to it, but without reciprocation the balance tips from two adults taking pleasure from each other, to one adult servicing and the other taking pleasure for both. In the realm of intimacy, sexual and otherwise, to give and not to get is paradoxically selfish.

CASE STUDY
Meet Grant

Grant came to see me because his sexual unselfishness is problematic for his partner. With a tinge of incredulity in his voice, he shares that his partner wants him to get better at taking a more receptive role in this bedroom instead of acting on his usual "all about you" attitude. He doesn't understand how it could be such a problem to anyone that he wants to make sure his partner is satisfied above and before all else. After all, he has always heard that being selfish in bed is unattractive and outright rude. But, since he really wants to be with his partner forever, he is willing to make some changes, even if it means going against his natural tendencies.

Grant is a giver in the bedroom. He gets off on "giving off." When he is with a partner, his greatest pleasure is seeing the pleasure his sexual partner receives from his efforts. He feels most aroused when his partner reaches their peak of ecstasy. He is proud of his abilities to bring other's sexual fulfillment, in most cases, and wants to bring the person he loves to orgasm often. He explained that it had been one of the reasons he thought his partner had stayed with him even through their tough times.

The best sexual experience of his life didn't even include his own orgasm. He was able to bring his then partner to orgasm 4 times in one evening. He recalls with a sly grin and puffed-up chest that his reputation preceded him in dating and had helped him to have his pick of partners.

Grant came to see me because his current partner feels like Grant isn't open to putting Grant first in the bedroom and he worries that it will be a source of resentment. His aim is to please, but he is beginning to realize that he doesn't have a lot of experience by way of connecting outside of ensuring his partners reach climax.

Grant's Intimacy Style is Giving. When he is engaging in any sexual activity with a partner, he prioritizes his partner's pleasure over anything else. After his mission is accomplished, he gets his kicks from being able to look at his partner basking in the afterglow and say to himself, "I did that." His sexual generosity has become a crutch in romantic relationships. I explained to Grant that if he continues to shut out his partner's attempts at reciprocating in the bedroom, he will miss out on the other relationship benefits of sex in the future.

The key to rounding out his intimate connection with this or any future partner/s would be to put effort into experiencing all four of the Intimacy Style into each sexual experience. For Grant, the Giving Style comes naturally to him, so we focused on Bonding, Release, and Responsive Styles. For Bonding, I asked him to consider what would happen if he were to find out that any of his partners had lied about reaching orgasm even if only once because they felt pressured to meet his expectations. He hadn't realized that in striving to always please his partners, there was an equal expectation that they always be pleased by him. It created a dynamic that calls for reciprocity but at the expense of authenticity. For Release, I asked him to consider what it would be like for a partner whose Intimacy Style is also Giving to be with Grant. How could their needs be met when he was only concerned with his need to give? For Responsive, I asked Grant to slow down and allow his partner to direct their next sexual experience. He would not be allowed to focus on his partner's pleasure until his partner shared they were ready.

Like so many others who are committed to the work they do with me, Grant later shared with me that his partner felt a newfound hope that they would be able to avoid sexual resentment and that they both felt like they were now partners in intimacy. He came to realize that by "rounding out" his Intimacy Style, he could enjoy sexual interactions without putting pressure on his partner or himself. Ultimately, they were able to have sex with more frequency and with more confidence.

FOR THE PARTNERS OF THOSE WITH A GIVING INTIMACY STYLE:

Feeling as though your partner gives you too much attention or sexual gratification is a nice problem to have. But it can certainly leave you feeling guilty or perhaps frustrated, since your attempts to focus on them never seem to be accepted or adequate enough. It should help to know that the Giving Style is not lying when they say they get more pleasure out of giving you pleasure than they do receiving it.

That said, the Giving Style has made people pleasing into an art form. They sometimes seem like mind readers because they kind of are. They trained themselves early on to pay very close attention to body language and other cues that communicated what a person was thinking and feeling, and how they might act on it. This was done out of self-preservation--if they could attend to someone's feelings before they got out of control, they could protect themselves from being hurt. As a result, they are probably very good at reading you, and might seem to anticipate your needs before you're consciously aware of them. If you notice your partner catering to you in this way, you can gently assure them that you are capable of taking care of yourself and would feel more at ease if they didn't worry about you. When this happens in the bedroom, feel free to enjoy, but when sex is over, initiate gentle but direct communication about reciprocity.

Your partner probably needs to hear how much you also enjoy giving sexual pleasure. You can explain that the pleasure you get in receiving pleasure from them is diminished slightly by your inability to return the favor. They will still struggle with feelings of inadequacy if they're on the receiving end, so it will help to remind them in the moment that you're feeling pleasure. The Giving Style is especially fond of dirty talk and moaning, so feel free to incorporate both as you take over giving duties.

If the rate of sexual intimacy between you has lessened, or if there is conflict in your relationship, your partner will feel very anxious about it. They will want to fix things. They will most likely try harder to be more accommodating and if this doesn't work, they will feel extreme distress. They may not show that to you, but know that they are feeling it and need you to lower the heat. To create an atmosphere of safety, it will be important to adjust your tone and demeanor. Approach your partner with a generous and respectful spirit.

Your partner will also benefit from you "translating" your own moods for them by making them explicit. In other words, if you've had a hard day and feel tired, the Giving Style might interpret your facial and body expression to mean you're upset. It will help them if you say, "I know I seem off tonight, but I'm just tired." Or, if you *are* upset with them, be forthcoming about it without blaming them. If they can sense you're upset but you don't say anything, they will walk on eggshells. It will be hard for them to hear that you're upset with them, but if you remain calm and explain without criticizing and without angry body language, this will free them from worrying as much and trying to appease you.

Perhaps the most important thing you can do for them is to positively reinforce anything they do that is solely for their own pleasure and enjoyment, or any switch in focus to their own needs. Tell them you think it's sexy when they're doing something they like or they're good at. Tell them that when they respect their needs, it gives you permission to do the same. Because it will be true; when our partners take their own pleasure, we feel liberated to satisfy our own. When they hold back, we feel like it might be wrong or unfair to enjoy ourselves.

GIVING

Think about it:

Learning about your own Intimacy Style will benefit you enormously, but I also recommend reading about each Intimacy Style. You will gain a better understanding of your (potential) partner, and you'll also gain a new perspective. This perspective will help you integrate features of each Style into your own, allowing you to experience the full range of intimacy. It is my professional opinion that the healthiest Intimacy Style is a combination of all 4, amounting to 25% of each.

THE 4 INTIMACY STYLES

Chapter 11
The RESPONSIVE Intimacy Style

As social beings, we take our cues from each other and act accordingly. It's in our nature to mirror those we come into contact with. Experts consider this impulse to have had survival benefits for our primitive ancestors, and the discovery of mirror neurons in the brain have led researchers to determine that we're wired to experience the actions of others as if they were our own. The Responsive Style might have more of these neurons firing because their interest in

sex is almost entirely dependent on the actions of their partner.

The Responsive Style is often considered (even by themselves) to have a low libido or possibly to suffer from Hypoactive Sexual Desire Disorder (HSDD) and yet this Intimacy Style tends to feel desire just fine in the early stages of a relationship. Gradually, sometimes over months but usually a couple years, their desire drops off and they scramble to come up with explanations for it. In the case of women, the assigned culprits are often pregnancy, postpartum depression, or the stress that goes along with having and raising kids. In the case of men, erectile dysfunction is often blamed, or perhaps a pornography addiction that has created too strong an association between desire and non-partnered sex. In the case of either gender: stressful jobs, medical issues, an ailing relative or recent loss, a side effect of antidepressants or a hormone imbalance are often possibilities they consider.

Additionally, the Responsive Style tends to blame themselves. They might think to themselves: "I love my partner, and I want to *want* my partner...my partner wants sex, and it will be good for us..." and they will try in this way to talk themselves into it. But instead of feeling sexy, they feel guilty. They often believe they are "broken" but there's nothing wrong with them. Any one of the aforementioned issues may be a factor and should be ruled out, but what they think of as low libido, while technically correct--they experience low sexual desire and sexual desire=libido--is not the whole story. The problem is one of perception. "Low libido" is often believed to be an immutable trait like eye color. Yet we know that under the right conditions (such as the excitement of a new relationship), a formerly low libido can skew high.

I believe libido is flexible and sensitive to context; everyone will have occasion to experience the highs and lows no matter where they typically land on the spectrum. For example, a person with a high libido won't have very strong sexual urges while they're sick with the flu, or visiting their grandmother.

And then there's a person with low libido in the early stages of falling for someone. Suddenly, and throughout the "drunk in love" stage, they experience rocketing desire.

New Relationship Energy is a deluge that floods everyone with lust, including the Responsive Style. Researchers know from studying brain scans of the newly-in-love that the regions in the brain's reward system that switch on in their brains are the same that activate when a drug addict uses cocaine. And when these couples separate, they experience the same brain changes involved in cocaine withdrawal. Quite literally, early love is an addiction. So, perhaps it's no surprise that when the cravings that come with that initial burst of chemical activity trade places with the quieter condition of emotional intimacy (usually between 6 months to 2 years in), the Responsive Style's libido tends to dip. At this juncture, the Responsive Style tends to settle rather than struggle, but despite the fact that they like the familiarity of long-term monogamy, they might find themselves feeling bored.

Desire and commitment are difficult for anyone to master simultaneously, but this combination is especially out of reach for the Responsive style. They find safety in being committed to their partner, but are less likely to romanticize their partnership the way a Bonding Style does, and unlike the Bonding, Giving, and Release Styles, they are not as inclined to express love physically. Of all the Intimacy Styles, they may experience the harshest effects of coming down from their early love high because their partner-addiction facilitated their desire. The Responsive Style longs for the feelings they had in the beginning when their partner easily lit them up.

For all of us, regardless of Intimacy Style, feeling hot and bothered is a process involving two components: arousal and desire. Most people think these are the same thing, but arousal refers to the physical feeling of being turned on, and desire is the mental part of it. The Responsive Style's feelings of arousal and desire are exogenous, which is to say, if their partner never suggested sex, they might never think of it. If their partner never touched them sensually, they might never feel arousal. If their partner never seduced them, they might never feel desire.

The Responsive Style experiences, fittingly, a kind of desire called "responsive desire." Responsive desire is the opposite of what our culture considers "natural." Somehow, we all got the message that desire is a sudden and powerful wanting that shows up without warning and overtakes you. According to the research, this is how the majority of men experience desire, but the majority of women experience either the inverse, or a combination. As I mentioned in Chapter 2, the reality for 5% of men and 30% of women is that sexual urges do not "just happen." They cannot access feelings of arousal any time or anywhere, and thoughts of sex don't often cause an immediate physical response. Sort of how thoughts about a heaping bowl of spaghetti wouldn't cue your appetite if you weren't a huge fan of pasta. The only difference is the Responsive Style can and very often does enjoy sex. So maybe it's more like: you *are* a pasta lover and a heaping bowl of spaghetti *will* make you ravenous given enough time...you just have a slower hunger response. And you might need to smell or taste it first in order to want it.

Likewise, the Responsive Style tends to feel the heat of desire by degree, sort of like a tea kettle reaching a boiling point. A tea kettle on the stove may not have any detectable response to flames under the burner for what feels like an eternity of waiting and watching...until finally you hear the bubbles quake and coalesce and the low drawn out note that signals it's about to explode into a shrill whistle. The Responsive Style's desire can seem just as sudden and explosive but just like the tea kettle, they need heat plus time. Those who experience spontaneous desire are more like pots on a continuous low simmer that can quickly come to a boil when the heat's turned up, and often the partners of the Responsive Style fit into that category. Simmering pots have difficulty intuitively understanding cold tea kettle. They're often impatient with the tea kettle's wait time. It helps if these partners of the Responsive Style shift their perspective to see it's not about the waiting (a watched tea kettle never boils); it's about building anticipation.

Spontaneous desire--the kind of desire we tend to see as "natural"--is really just a tendency to take something sexually "relevant" and piece it together with their subjective experience of arousal and desire. In other words, something sex-related happens or appears (in the world or in their brains), and they get turned on. You know how when something catches your attention and suddenly you start seeing it everywhere? It's the "blue car syndrome," also known as frequency illusion. You're in the market for a new car. You decide to buy a blue car so you can stand out from the crowd and now you see blue cars everywhere you go. Those with spontaneous desire find themselves surrounded by blue cars (or, sexually relevant stimuli). Every blue car reinforces their original interest in blue cars and then they start to think about them and how much they want their own blue car. The Responsive Style notices the occasional blue car, but blue cars haven't been on their mind, so the blue car sighting doesn't get integrated into their subjective experience. They need someone or something else to make the blue car relevant.

Perhaps because of this, the partners of the Responsive Style often complain that the Responsive Style never initiates. These partners may need to accept that the Responsive Style never will, except out of obligation (and who wants that?). But this doesn't necessarily mean that they don't want to have sex. The Responsive Style can acknowledge they enjoy sex when they have it, and they also recognize the benefits of sex and know intellectually they want to experience them with their partner. But it's likely they're a tea kettle sitting on a cold burner with a partner who doesn't realize they need heat (a lot of it)...or, how to turn it on. And, typically, the Responsive Style doesn't know how to either.

The Responsive style is often partnered with one of the other 3 Intimacy Styles which complicates things. A Bonding partner will feel unloved by them, a Release partner will feel frustrated by them, and a Giving partner will feel unneeded by them. The Responsive style will feel guilty but also resent any of the 3 for expecting them to perform sexually (as they see it) at the drop of a hat.

You see, heat plus time are necessary, but so is context. The Responsive Style is sensitive to their environment, their state of mind, and the state of their relationships. If one of these is off, say, the sheets are dirty, or they're preoccupied with an emotional or logistical problem, or they just had a fight with their partner, there's no way they're going to see or appreciate any blue cars. The context they require is specific to them, (maybe they don't care about the sheets, but they can't relax until they send a work email) and the partners of the Responsive Style need to develop an awareness of these particular stressors to guide them in figuring out what needs to be handled before they initiate.

So that's clearing away the stressors and improving the context, but what exactly is their source of heat, and how does it get turned on? The list varies depending on the individual but in general the Responsive Style enjoys being seduced over a period of time--usually a few hours to a few days--and the following are some examples of bids that tend to work:

- A positive and confident attitude from their partner
- Suggestive flirting
- Periodic sexting throughout the day
- Cuddling with no expectation of sex
- Neck kisses
- Massage
- Their partner communicating how desirable they find them
- Going on a date
- Romantic notes
- Tidying the house

You might notice that with the exception of tidying up, this list includes all of the behaviors that were present in the beginning of a relationship. That's not a coincidence. The Responsive Style "responds" even in the beginning but neither they nor their partner noticed because there was so much to respond *to*. Again, the list varies depending on the individual so the Responsive Style needs to contemplate what they responded to in the beginning, and whether or not it can be replicated in the present. It will help to write down their list so both they and their partner can reference it later.

The Responsive style also needs some kind of physical charge in addition to the romantic inspiration listed above. Arousal doesn't start in their imagination unless they purposely conjure sexual images, and even then, they aren't always able to anticipate pleasure. Often their partners worry they're not attracted to them, and this typically comes as a surprise to the Responsive Style, who doesn't find lust to be a necessary component to feeling attraction. They can acknowledge they find their partner's looks or body sexually attractive, just as they can acknowledge their favorite meal is appetizing, but if they're not currently hungry, they won't have any desire to consume it. Just like the physical senses involved in smelling or tasting their favorite meal could trigger their appetite, the Responsive Style needs something to physically trigger their arousal before they can become aware of desire.

Pulling from the aforementioned list, some options might be massage, cuddling, or neck kisses. This can present a chicken or the egg dilemma however, in which the Responsive Style is not in the mood for physical affection, but physical affection is what they need to have a physical response powerful enough to activate desire. So, here's the thing: The Responsive Style has to accept that unlike the other Intimacy Styles, they need to be intentional. They can't wait until they're driven mad by lust-unless their partner gets them going, that may never happen. They have to *want* to want to.

Ultimately, the Responsive Style needs to reserve the time to relax, enjoy their partner's touch, and let whatever happens happen--much like they did in the beginning of their relationship. Scheduling a "Netflix and Chill" session kills two birds with one stone: they'll know ahead of time to take care of context, and the anticipation of sex will get them in the right state of mind.

The Responsive Style will often say that they can only get into sex once they're already *having* sex. If they know this about themselves, they can take the "just do it" approach which means, barring any physical or emotional stress, they give a default "yes" to their partner's initiations. But something else they can try is a "just think about it" approach. It will take conscious deliberation and a certain mindfulness to think about sex throughout the day, and initially it may feel like it's not working, but the more the Responsive Style intends to think about sex, the more their brain will automatically land on sexual thoughts. They will start to see blue cars.

Sometimes cultural messages play a role in the Responsive Style's ability to feel desire. It's similar to the way most men are socialized not to cry. As if to demonstrate the efficacy of this socialized message, most men are desensitized to emotional stimuli that might trigger crying, and even if they suffer a terrible blow, some will find they're physically unable to produce tears. They can acknowledge their sorrow, and sometimes feel tears welling up--sometimes they even *want* to cry--and yet they find that they can't. This is close to what the Responsive Style experiences when they try to invoke sexual urges.

As I've already touched on throughout this book, we've all gotten messages that sexual urges are uncivilized, disgusting, and inappropriate. Girls tend to receive a harsher and more punitive message, while boys are offered a loophole in which "boys will be boys." But that isn't to say we don't still treat boys like animals for having sexual impulses, because we absolutely do. Boys will be boys translates to boys can't help themselves which ultimately means boys are like animals. Girls on the other hand, are supposed to be above animal weakness, and are *never* to develop an appetite for sex. It is often difficult, even terrifying, for grown-up women in monogamous relationships to admit they like sex. And depending on whether or not an early caregiver had negative views of sexual behavior and required unswerving loyalty, boys may become men who also have a slower sexual response and can't openly communicate about sex. These two will almost certainly fit into the Responsive Style and only experience responsive desire.

There is safety in responding. The Responsive Style doesn't have to claim ownership of the sexual urge, nor do they have to claim sex as their idea. It doesn't matter that they're typically responding inside the walls of their own home or to a committed partner and no one else is witness to it. They internalized shame about sexual impulses at a time when they had very little "theory of mind," or an ability to understand that other people are not experiencing and thinking about the same things we are--without theory of mind, they believed their shaming caregiver (or other shaming influence) was aware of their thoughts and experienced everything with them, like an omniscient being. Fast forward to adulthood, and the internalized shame--frozen at this stage of development and now buried and unconscious--makes them feel as though they're being monitored at all times for evidence of sexual behavior. And in a way they are. Their executive function, situated in their frontal lobes, is an inner voice that took over from parents or caregivers, and usually this voice produces guidance and admonishment in just the same way their caregivers once did. Talk about a buzzkill.

When their partner is the one to initiate, they can assign "blame" to their partner. Sometimes this means they get to enjoy sex, knowing they had to be "talked into it" and "won over," and sometimes it means they're irrationally angry at their partner for daring to act on an impermissible craving. In the case of a woman who is a Responsive Style, there may be additional complicated narratives hijacking her response...

messages like: "Don't give it up, your partner will lose respect for you!" Or, "Your only value is between your legs, so you need to carefully guard it." Or my least favorite: "[your partner] won't buy the cow if the milk is free." These messages don't have to be consciously accepted to hold power, or even relevant (in the case of a monogamous partnership, let's assume your partner "bought the cow"). They have instead bubbled up to the surface of consciousness as rationalizations, like: "I'm just not a sexual person." Or "I could go the rest of my life without sex." Go the rest of your life not being tortured by your beaten-down desire to have sex? Well, that does sound ideal when you put it that way.

The thing is, we all experience responsive desire. We're all responding to something, be it direct stimulation, an attractive stranger, our partner, or a transient thought. Arousal, or the physical manifestation of sex drive, can be experienced randomly without any direct cause (such is the case with "morning wood"), but desire (the mental state in which we want sex) always has some preliminary feeling or trigger attached. Yet we seem to have a romanticized ideal of desire in which the impulse strikes like lightning and suddenly we want it, and we want it bad. The problem with this ideal is that the Responsive Style typically believes that unless they're filled with longing and raring to go, sex is not an option. But if they're waiting until they experience romance novel throbbing and heaving, they're never going to have sex. It's more like you have two coworkers in neighboring cubicles. One of them is more motivated to go grab a cookie from the break room--the other could take it or leave it. But when the first brings back cookies for both of them, the second thinks "that does look good" and eats the whole cookie. Were they swooning at the very thought of a cookie? No, but they ended up enjoying it anyway. The Responsive Style should not feel that they are defective just because they aren't motivated by the very thought of sex.

The Responsive Style will evolve to be more comfortable with wanting sex if they feel their partner is understanding and willing to put time and effort into seducing them. And if they "just do it," so to speak, they may find as time goes on that the more sex they have, the more they want sex. It's almost as if having sex reminds the Responsive Style that it's enjoyable. They tend to experience aftershocks of desire afterward that can last up to a couple of days, so in some cases, the best time to initiate sex with the Responsive Style is hours after having sex or the following day. And mini-sex-marathons will increase intimacy in their relationship and help their partner feel validated. As inspiration, I recommend the Responsive Style shift their mindset to regard sex as self-care.

The Responsive Intimacy Style has the most potential for growth because typically they have their own inner drive for sex. In fact, they typically quite like sex...they simply need to set the intention, practice accepting their partner's initiation, practice thinking about it, and allow themselves to feel connected to the sensations they were long ago cut off from. They might always have responsive desire in the sense that they're dependent on their partner to "bring them sex" as if they were bringing flowers, but there's nothing wrong with that. Sex motivates everyone somehow, and the motivations change depending on the Intimacy Style. For the Responsive Style, the motive may not be physical (at first) and that's ok. It's ok to set an intention rather than be set ablaze by passion. They may find that their libido is just fine, and that all they need is a plan to be physical, a partner who provides the right context and inspiration, and a little patience.

CASE STUDIES

Meet Rebecca

Rebecca came to see me because her spouse urged her to figure out why she isn't ever one to initiate or even show any real enthusiasm toward physical intimacy. They have sex, good sex at that, but it's rarely ever because of Rebecca. She shrugged her shoulders and said, "Sex is really fun when it's happening, but I'm not, like, fantasizing about it all day or begging for it or anything." She can't quite understand why her partner expects her to "be horny all the time." Rebecca goes on to share that they've often discussed the differences in the way they feel about sex in their relationship, but now they have been having more and more arguments over sex.

Truth is, Rebecca could live without ever having sex again. She doesn't like to admit it but it's true. She doesn't have sexual urges often and when she does, a quick solo session with her battery-operated adult accessory can do the trick just as well as a romp with her spouse. She appreciates that for others "sex is such a big deal" but it just isn't for her. Rebecca really only wants to be intimate if/when her partner does. She came to see me because her lack of enthusiasm for sex hurts her spouse's feelings, and she would like to know what is "wrong" with her. Rebecca's Intimacy Style is Responsive. When she engages in any sexual activity with a partner, she hopes that it will fulfill her partner's needs for intimacy. She feels closer to her spouse when they are physically intimate and she enjoys the connection it brings after it has occurred, but she doesn't need to scratch that itch otherwise. She is inadvertently leaving her spouse feeling uninspired and, even worse, undesired by their one-sided sex life, hurting their chances at long lasting intimacy. If Rebecca continues to engage in sexuality solely for the purpose of satisfying her partner's attempts, she will miss out on the other relationship benefits of sex.

The key to rounding out her intimate connection with her spouse would be to put effort into experiencing all four of the Intimacy Styles with each sexual interaction. For Rebecca, the Responsive Style comes naturally to her, so we focused on Bonding, Release, and Giving Styles. For Bonding, I asked her to consider just how insecure she would feel if her spouse showed as little interest in wanting her sexually as she does. She has taken it for granted for so long that she is the object of their affection without giving any thought to her spouse not getting the same attention. This lack of desirability can erode even the most loving connection. For Release, I asked Rebecca what her spouse does to her body that gets her excited in a sexual interaction and asked her to fantasize at least once per week about that stimulation and subsequent arousal. For Giving, I asked her to make sure to hold her partner close and share how grateful she feels to have their love and thank them for carrying the torch for their sex life thus far.

Like so many others who are committed to the work they do with me, Rebecca realized that if she wanted to keep the love life she had cherished so much, she would need to put some effort into creating her own level of healthy motivation for sex in their marriage and act on it. She realized that by "rounding out" her Intimacy Style, she could enjoy sexual interactions with more frequency and enthusiasm. This has allowed her to get much more out of their physical intimacy than ever before.

FOR THE PARTNERS OF THOSE WITH
A RESPONSIVE INTIMACY STYLE:

Imagine you're at a resort with your partner. They schedule a couple's massage and tell you they can't wait to have this experience with you. You're not really a massage person and would never think to book one on your own time, but you're happy they're happy and you think to yourself, why not--there's nothing wrong with a little relaxation. You go along and have a good time. Now replace massage with sex, and you know how it feels for the Responsive Style to have sex with their partner. They wouldn't think to initiate sex on their own, but because you want to, they'll accept your invitation and likely end up having a good time.

Or at least, this is how it tends to work until the initiating partner (you) develops resentment for having to be the only one to initiate. Which is understandable. You want your partner to be equally enthused about "massages" and book them on their own every once in a while. You may have asked your partner to initiate more, and they may have promised to do so and yet you've been disappointed by their relatively few attempts. So, what's the disconnect? Let's try another metaphor.

I don't usually buy champagne when I go grocery shopping. But I will grab a glass if it's offered at a party. I will happily take a refill when offered. But after the party, I never even think about champagne. If I see it in the store, I don't light up the way I do when I'm in a good mood and at a party surrounded by my friends. I associate the drink with the celebratory occasion. The champagne at the store is not part of a festive spread and somehow it seems less appealing to get it myself. It's the same drink, but the motivation and context is different. Sex is similar for the Responsive Style. In the right mood, sex is exciting when it's offered, but they don't feel compelled to seek it out for themselves. It's not an insult, and there's nothing wrong with you as a partner.

To be the partner of a Responsive Style means developing an awareness and understanding that they do not *want* to avoid intimacy with you. And it doesn't mean tolerating no sex. The Responsive Style just needs a push. Sometimes all they need is for you to initiate--to "book the massage" or "offer the champagne." And sometimes they need a little more.

Consider the effort you made in the beginning of your relationship to flirt with your partner. I'm willing to bet there were hundreds of phone calls, texts, emails, snapchats--whatever medium for communication you used, the flirty messages were probably bountiful. The flirting gave your partner context--a headspace in which they felt admired, wanted, and excited--which you likely then followed with time spent together and during this time you probably kissed or full on made out. As a result, your partner had context and heat. And I imagine these moments were more drawn out than they tend to be now. Sure, the beginning of your relationship probably calls up memories of frantic undressing and gotta-have-it sex, but think of the gazing and the touching that led up to it. Dates together were probably pleasurable and unbearable all at once. To have to sit in a restaurant? Through a whole movie? When all you wanted was to ravish each other? Every moment was filled with heat, and you turned it up slowly by each exquisitely agonizing degree. *How's that for initiation?*

You may scoff at the following suggestion, especially in light of what I just reminded you of but trust me: *schedule sex.* Which is to say, choose a couple days and times per week to engage in sexual activity that are mutually agreeable to you and your partner. This arrangement is beneficial for you both. You don't have to initiate (and risk rejection), and they don't have to experience a rough transition from not wanting sex to making themselves try. Don't think of it as an assignment or an appointment because it's neither. It's context. Which is to say, it's *a date*.

I don't recommend meeting up in the bedroom at a specific time on a specific day to go through the motions. I want you to flirt with your partner during the day leading up to the scheduled time, and then I want you to "take them on a date." Either literally, as in leaving the house and enjoying some quality time, or by just reserving some time to do something simple like watch a movie or share a cheese plate and talk about your day. And sure, you might be on the couch, which you share, in the residence you both live in, but that doesn't make this any less of an opportunity to make the moves you once did. By refraining from rushing to bed you're giving your partner time to stay suspended in anticipation of it, which is to say, time to warm up. This is the most important, yet often overlooked step to seducing the Responsive Style.

The next most important step is foreplay. Earlier in the book I outlined how important "extended" foreplay is, and I'll repeat here for emphasis that foreplay starts as soon as the last sexual interaction ends. In other words, getting your partner in the mood should be a dedicated and ongoing effort. The actual physical foreplay that occurs before intercourse is also of extreme importance to the Responsive Style. They need much more than passionate kissing to get them to peak arousal. I recommend asking your partner what feels good to them in as much detail as possible. Ask about what kind of touch they like, their preferred speed or pressure, and what areas they want you to focus on. Regardless of their specific preferences, it's usually a good idea to build their anticipation with teasing. Teasing slows the pace and provides the good kind of tension. Be sure to keep this interaction playful; don't exert control over their body unless your partner has given you a mutually agreed upon direction to do so.

Your partner needs to be intentional about creating the space and time to relax and enjoy sensual activity, and your help and patience in this endeavor will be critical to their success. Simply offering your understanding of their Intimacy Style and experience of desire will go far in establishing trust between you as you work on your intimate connection. In general, it helps to remain confident and lighthearted; nothing turns off a Responsive Style quicker than a partner who's sulky, needy, or picking fights. The Responsive Style tends to feel guilty for experiencing desire differently from their partner, and any conflict it causes will only raise their defenses.

I've asked your partner to write a list of their sexual "triggers" and to share these with you. Let this list be your guide to creating context and motivation for your partner. I would also recommend you and your partner do some of the somatic and/or sensate focus exercises in The Dr. Viviana Method for Intimate Reconnection©. Both of you are probably in need of a physical reset with each other. Slowing down and focusing on the intimacy of physical pleasure will set the stage for great sex.

To review: your partner feels misunderstood and anxious, and needs you to put yourself in their shoes and look at sex (particularly initiation) from their perspective. They need to feel that you understand them and that you'll be patient with them as you both explore what triggers them sexually. Try to recall what you did in the beginning of your relationship that stirred their desire and ask them to share their list with you. Schedule sex. To create motivation for your partner, you need to actively "date" or seduce them on the days you've agreed to have sexual contact. Provide foreplay both outside and inside the bedroom to give them context, heat, and time. Remember that your partner wants intimacy with you, but they need you to blatantly express your desire for them, and to feel comfortable being the one to initiate.

THE 4 INTIMACY STYLES

Part IV

ROUNDING OUT YOUR INTIMACY STYLE

"Sexual incompatibility is a myth."

- DR. VIVIANA

Chapter 12
Intimacy Styles Challenges and Tips

By now you should have some idea what your Intimacy Style is. It's possible more than one Intimacy Style spoke to you, in which case you're a blend of Intimacy Styles. This is common. You have also likely identified your partner in the descriptions of Intimacy Styles and have gained a deeper appreciation for the ways they experience and express intimacy. Hopefully you have gained a deeper appreciation of yourself as well.

Now is the time to lean in to a purposeful shift. As I mentioned elsewhere in the book, I recommend my clients adopt traits of *all* Intimacy Styles to round out their own. The reason for this is simple: when you limit yourself to experiencing intimacy only through your own particular Style, you're only bringing a fourth of your potential resources to the experience of intimacy. If your partner's Style differs from your own (and most partners will have different Styles), you're denying yourself and them the opportunity to bond through your differences and integrate them.

If your partner grew up in another culture, you would likely welcome their traditions and customs into your home and your lives together. If the language they spoke with their family of origin differed from yours, you might try to learn it. You might integrate their holiday traditions into your own to form new traditions you share together. If their culture involved religious or ideological beliefs, you might observe their rituals or simply respect and make space for them to practice these. Intimacy Styles are the same. In order to honor your partner's experience of intimacy, you must welcome and integrate it into your shared intimate life.

A difference in Intimacy Styles could be viewed by couples as a fundamental sexual incompatibility. "Sexual incompatibility" is a term that is often considered an irreversible condition and a deal-breaker for relationships. It doesn't have to be, but this defeatist attitude is one I often see from the couples I counsel. "Incompatibility" is often a simple case of sexual disconnection. It is what happens when a couple stops turning toward each other, and each directs their energy and focus to other aspects of their lives. While it's true that no human being can sustain the intensity of falling in love and the obsessive attention they devote to a partner in the early days of their relationship--no one has the molecular resources to withstand the deprivation of sleep and lack of appetite symptomatic of "lovesickness"--a complete redirection of romantic energy will inevitably lead to partners living as roommates. Roommates may get along well enough, but they are, by definition, sexually incompatible.

Somewhere along the way, these couples exited what was once automatic and entered a phase that demanded intention.

All couples make this transition, but some will expect sex to remain automatic, spontaneous, and all-consuming and won't replace these unsustainable conditions with intention, either because they don't realize they need to, or because they believe the myth that sexual compatibility is a mystery of chemistry and you either have it or you don't. They believe if you have to force it, it's not real. These couples often make assumptions about what they're each thinking or experiencing and don't set aside the time to explore their differences with an open mind. They might believe they've grown apart and that's that. When really, they need to meet each other all over again. Their sexual disconnection is an opportunity to start dating again; to figure each other out as sexual beings in a latter phase of romantic attachment.

On the other hand, whether or not they know it, the healthiest couples navigate intimate disconnection using the knowledge they have of each other's Intimacy Style. These couples are masters of each other's Style because they have taken the time to learn how they each experience pleasure, attachment, and intimacy. These couples regularly communicate their desire for each other through their actions, words, and touch. They don't take chances, or take each other for granted. Rather than make assumptions, they feel responsible for making sure their partner knows how they feel. They would never think, "Oh, my partner knows I'm committed to them, I don't need to express an attraction to them." They're explicit in their appreciation for each other, and feel safe discussing their concerns. When they face challenges, these couples make every effort to understand what's going on. They don't view these challenges as their partner's problem or their own; they take them on together. In fact, they don't necessarily view conflict as negative. They see conflict as an opportunity to analyze the problem and grow from it.

These couples are also naturally curious about each other, and though they have an expansive and deep relationship, they feel there is always more to discover. These couples know that love and sex change over the years, and that they and their partner change with them. They're eager to keep up to date with each other's shifting attitudes and beliefs, some of which might inspire a shift in their experience of intimacy. They don't need to "spice up" the relationship, because their interest in each other takes care of that. As opposed to couples who mourn the passing of NRE (New Relationship Energy), and long to get it back, these couples feel their current relationship is far more satisfying. Time has only strengthened their bond. They feel their relationship has far more dimension than it did, and believe it has the potential to get even better as more time goes by.

This sense of curiosity and excitement is how you should approach an understanding of your partner's Intimacy Style and how it intersects with your own. The two of you should take pleasure in learning something new about each other and enjoy the process of expanding your individual Styles to include traits of all 4. You'll not only gain a feel for what your partner experiences, you'll develop mastery of intimacy as a whole. On that note, let's go through each Style and find habits and routines that allow us to experience the benefits of each.

Before a Sexual Experience:

- Share how much you are looking forward to your sexy time together
- Send an "I love you" text
- Light candles
- Remove distractions- no screens, get a babysitter, put the dogs outside, put your phone on Do Not Disturb mode
- Send a picture of a fond memory you have with your partner

During a Sexual Experience:

- Make eye contact
- Read Erotic literature to each other
- Kiss deeply
- Play a specially curated music playlist
- Read love poems
- Take turns sharing fantasies

After a Sexual Experience:

- Compliment your partner on their attentiveness
- Let your partner know what felt good
- Hug and cuddle
- Say (and mean) that you can't wait until you get to
- do it again soon
- Get up and go on a walk together

IF YOU NEED TO INCORPORATE MORE OF THE RELEASE STYLE INTO YOUR SEX LIFE:

Before a Sexual Experience:

- Grab some lubricant
- Have your favorite adult toy on hand
- Stretch your limbs
- Make sure you are groomed to your liking
- Write a letter, text, or email about the things you want your partner to do to you.

During a Sexual Experience:

- Solo pleasure if it enhances your experience
- Moan, groan, and vocalize without shame
- Take a break if you need it even if it's inconvenient for your partner
- Stay in the zone of your own pleasure. Feel free to "use" your partner for your own satisfaction
- Try a sexual act, prop, or position you've always wanted to

After a Sexual Experience:

- Enjoy the "high" of oxytocin and cuddle as long as you wish
- Make sure your toolkit is stocked and ready, and your toys are fully charged for your next rendezvous
- Journal a description of your experience so you can use it to fantasize
- Recap what worked best for you with your partner
- Ask for a Round 2 or go it alone

CHALLENGES AND TIPS

IF YOU NEED TO INCORPORATE MORE OF THE GIVING STYLE INTO YOUR SEX LIFE:

Before a Sexual Experience:

- Plan a romantic evening that involves your partner's favorite meal
- Share a letter with your partner about the things you want to do to them
- Draw a bath for your partner and let them soak
- Offer your partner a full body massage

During a Sexual Experience:

- Perform a sexual act that is meant to give only your partner
- pleasure (but allow yourself to be turned on by it too)
- Make intercourse as varied and enjoyable as possible by experimenting with different or new positions and pay attention to which of these your partner gets the most pleasure from
- Act out a fantasy of your partner's

After a Sexual Experience:

- Share what you enjoyed most about catering to your partner.
- Thank them for letting you please them
- Write down sexual activities, positions, toys, etc. that you want to use in the future to pleasure your partner and allow your partner to contribute to this list
- Ask your partner to share a letter of what they want to try in a future sexual experience. Encourage them to share a fantasy and plan how to carry it out

IF YOU NEED TO INCORPORATE MORE OF THE RESPONSIVE STYLE INTO YOUR SEX LIFE:

Before a Sexual Experience:

- Tackle your to-do list together to free your mind
- Allow your partner to plan out a sexual experience and enjoy going along for the ride
- Schedule your next time to get frisky
- Enjoy getting gradually turned on by your partner's efforts to arouse you
- Approach your scheduled sexual activities as self-care

During a Sexual Experience:

- Let your partner run the show by initiating and choosing what sexual acts or positions you try
- Allow yourself to simply absorb the sensations of sex without any need to control the outcome
- Act out a fantasy of your partner's
- Together, either act out or talk about a time before your relationship officially started and there was sexual attraction between you two--do to each other what you would have longed to do then

After a Sexual Experience:

- Take a shower together after
- Ask your partner to plan for a time where they take charge of a sexual situation. Be sure that you have communicated your limits beforehand
- Write another list of attributes your partner has that you find sexy. Include physical attributes, as well as things they do or say that turn you on

Be prepared to experience some resistance when you first incorporate different Intimacy Styles into your sex life. Your partner may express reluctance, and you may question whether or not this experiment is worthwhile. The way we each approach sex usually involves identifying beliefs, and often our relationships have taken shape around these beliefs. Someone who identifies as a Giving Style may struggle to seek Release in their partner. Someone who identifies as Responsive may find it uncomfortable to express love through sex and enjoy the closeness required in the Bonding Style.

When you've grown comfortable in your sexual habits with a partner (even if you're so comfortable, you experience boredom), it can feel vulnerable to experiment. I encourage you to push through your resistance. If you do, you'll make 4 valuable discoveries. First, you'll discover yourself, and learn what you most need from a partner and from sex in order to feel fulfilled. Then you'll discover how your partner experiences intimacy, and learn how to provide for their needs. This will lead to you and your partner discovering how to integrate each other's Style into a mutually satisfying sex life. Finally, you'll learn how you and your partner interact as you take turns experimenting with each Intimacy Style. If you progress through each stage one by one, you'll find that any trepidation you feel will melt away. You will finally feel understood by your partner as you both learn to embrace each other's natural Styles, leading to the greatest intimacy you have ever experienced.

THE 4 INTIMACY STYLES

DISCUSSION QUESTIONS

With your partner or in a group setting, I encourage you to continue the sexual communication.

Here are some conversation starters:

1. What messages did you get about sex growing up?
2. Which messages have shaped the way you feel about intimacy as an adult?
3. What sexual myths have you heard? Were they debunked?
4. What is your definition of Intimacy?
5. What is your definition of Love?
6. Why is Sex important in a long-term committed relationship?
7. What can couples do to make sure they're connecting sensually?
8. Is it easier for you to be physically or emotionally intimate, and why?
9. How can relationships benefit when both partners know their Intimacy Style?
10. How did your Intimacy styles develop?
11. How can you honor your partner's Intimacy Style?
12. What's your plan to round out your Intimacy Style?
13. Are you prioritizing anything over your partner, and what can you change to make sure your partner is the priority?
14. What can you do for your partner that can be considered "foreplay outside the bedroom?"
15. How can you improve your sexual communication with your partner?

THE 4 INTIMACY STYLES

PERSONAL THOUGHTS

_____

_____

_____

_____

_____

_____

_____

_____

_____

_____

_____

_____

_____

PERSONAL THOUGHTS

NOTES

https://www.healthline.com/health/healthy-sex-health-benefits#in-men-and-women Sex make us healthier, physically and mentally, 14.

The Show About Something: Anxious Manhood and Homosocial Order on Seinfeld Joanna L. Dimattia vol. 14, 1999-2000 Issue Title: Masculinities, 15.

https://www.scientificamerican.com/article/daydreaming-may-help-you-become-more-socially-adept/The brain's default mode, 18.

https://link.springer.com/article/10.1007/s10902-018-0057-1 Higher committed relationships lead to greater life satisfaction, 27.

https://www.psychologytoday.com/us/blog/hide-and-seek/201706/are-married-people-healthier The health benefits of marriage and long term partnership, 19.

https://journals.sagepub.com/doi/10.1111/j.1467 9280.2006.01832.x Study of married women whose levels of cortisol lower when they're holding their husband's hand, 19.

https://ifstudies.org/blog/the-share-of-never-married-americans-has-reached-a-new-high Pew research center never marrieds, 24.

https://www.theledger.com/entertainmentlife/20190329/dear-abby-intimacy-tank-on-empty-as-dog-gets-more-affection-in-loveless-marriage Dear Abby letter, 32.

https://thoughtcatalog.com/christopher-hudspeth/2013/11/15-signs-your-significant-other-loves-a-pet-more-than-they-love-you/, 32.

https://www.psychologytoday.com/us/blog/meet-catch-and-keep/201401/5-reasons-why-couples-who-sweat-together-stay-together Physical exercise with a partner proven to create positive associations; couples mirror each other through nonverbal mimicry, 46.

https://www.healthline.com/health/healthy-sex/sexless-marriage Statistics on sexless marriage, 67.

BIBLIOGRAPHY

Bergner, D. (2013). *What do women want?* Edinburgh[u.a.]: Canongate Books.

Berman, L. *The passion prescription: Ten weeks to your best sex--ever.* New York: Hachette Books.

Briggs, D. C. (1967). *Your child's self-esteem.* New York: Doubleday.

Chapman, G., Campbell, R., & Southern, R. (2016). *The 5 love languages.* Chicago: Moody Publishers.

Coles, V. A. (2021). *The Dr. Viviana Method for Intimate Reconnection.* Houston: Viviana A. Coles.

Hendrix, H., & Hunt, H. L. (2003). *Getting the love you want workbook* New York: Atria Books.

Martin, W. (2018). *Untrue.* New York: Little, Brown Spark, an imprint of Little, Brown and Company.

Nagoski, E. (2015). *Come as you are.* New York: Simon & Schuster Paperbacks.

Perel, E. (2007). *Mating in captivity: Unlocking erotic intelligence.* London: Yellow Kite.

Perel, E. (2017). *The state of affairs: Rethinking infidelity.* New York: Harper Books.

Ryan, C., & Jethá, C. (2011). *Sex at dawn.* New York: Harper Perennial.

Schnarch, D. (1997). *Passionate marriage.* New York: Norton.

Shapiro, F. R. (2006). *The Yale book of quotations.* New Haven: Yale Univ. Press.

van der Kolk, B. (2014). *The body keeps the score.* East Rutherford: Penguin Publishing Group.

ACKNOWLEDGEMENTS

Writing a book, I've come to find, is so much more than the writing of the book. Particularly in my case, because I made the decision at the onset that I would be professionally self-publishing my first book. I never doubted that decision even when approached with the opportunity to go the traditional route. In fact, the more research (a ton- all day, every day) I did, the more I knew professionally self-publishing was the right path for me, a control-fiend and businesswoman. The more I learned, the more I craved taking this endeavor independently. But I also recognize that the reason I was able to remain steadfast in my pursuit is because I am surrounded by so many talented women with the skill sets to make amazing accomplishments happen! This is a very concise list, but know that it truly took a community of intelligent, capable, boss ladies to help me get this to you.

Taylor- you are my right-hand woman and you know I couldn't have done any of this without your make-it-happen attitude and no-holds-barred work ethic. Personally and professionally, you have given me the absolute gift of being able to know that, under your management, Houston Relationship Therapy is in good hands while I'm away filming, on vacation, on TV, speaking engagements, kids' sports games, radio appearances, etc. Houston Relationship Therapy continues to grow exponentially every year and it's all possible because of you!

The team at Houston Relationship Therapy- you ladies are total rockstars! Your clients know it, I know it, and I hope you know it. You continue to exceed my expectations and I am so grateful for your loyalty and hard work. HRT has a stellar reputation and it's because you are amazing!

Jori- Well, we did it! You should be so proud of how incredibly gorgeous you have made this book and accompanying website. You and I have been working together for a very long time and I appreciate the way you have cultivated my digital image in a world where I am a "brand." Thank you for always being available for this very needy client and for always promising to "figure it out" for me. You truly are a multi-hyphenate boss mama (of 3 as of publication date)!

Juliana- You have made my professional growing pains so much less painful! You have an almost superhuman ability to talk me down when all of my ideas and dreams and concerns are threatening to slow me down. And while I know this wasn't the first book idea we talked through, the other books are coming as long as you are able to fit me in for last-minute executive coaching sessions. Thank you for reminding me that I own the land, so there's no need to rent.

Lauren- I love that you have a special interest in this topic and that you were so eager to jump right in and help me to get my thoughts out on paper. May I be so forward as to imply that your coaching me through the writing process was meant to be? We were able to quickly get intimate about intimacy and it just goes to show that meeting someone through someone you trust really does lead to the best of relationships, working or otherwise!

Paria- Thank you for your affirmations and for empowering me to trust my vision and plan for this book. While you may prefer to work behind the scenes, I hope you know you always have a seat at the table. Thank you for making this new world in the media so much less stressful and foreign for me.

All of My Clients- Without the experiences I've had with my clients at Houston Relationship Therapy, this book would not exist. Y'all have given me the opportunity to positively impact future generations through your openness and vulnerability. Sharing your intimate moments with me has enriched my practice as a psychotherapist and relationship expert. I will forever cherish and be grateful for our interactions.

Vanessa, Tiffanie, and Lauren- Thank you for being a source of comfort and hilarity as my career takes me away from home more and more often. I cherish our friendship and your willingness to mom so hard on my behalf whenever needed. #mafiamoms

Angel, Robert, and Andrea- You have single-handedly ensured that I will never get a big head no matter what I accomplish and I love y'all for it! Your incessant trolling and demand for humility have prepared me for being under public scrutiny. For that, I thank you. Angel, thanks for being a beta reader and for always celebrating me.

Mom, Dad, and Julian- You have always been my biggest supporters. I'm so lucky that you have always been willing to jump in and help whenever I need it. You are the greatest parents and grandparents. Thank you for being my main source of inspiration when it comes to lasting emotional and physical intimacy in a marriage. Your loving connection is enviable and I love you both so much. Big bro Julian, thanks for not ever wanting to steal my spotlight. Amo.

My kiddos- Thank you for affording me the opportunity to fulfill this goal without the usual accompanying mom-guilt. Y'all are troopers! Thank you for always letting me know how proud of me you are and sometimes letting me know that you think I'm a "Cool Mom." Amo muco, cuties.

Bobby- You are my first love, my last love, and I am obsessed with you. Thank you for your undying care and support as I navigate this incredibly wild time in our lives. I'm so fortunate to have you in my heart and by my side. You are the best partner I could have ever hoped for. I love you and our family.

ABOUT THE AUTHOR

DR. VIVIANA COLES
Doctor of Marriage & Family Therapy,
Licensed Marriage & Family Therapist,
Certified Sex Therapist,
Media Relationship & Intimacy Expert,
Celebrity Therapist

Since 2003, Dr. Viviana Coles has exclusively focused on her work with couples and individuals experiencing emotional and physical intimacy issues in private practice at Houston Relationship Therapy where she and her team of hand-picked relationship and intimacy specialists see clients both in-person and virtually. Dr. Viviana has been featured as a relationship and sex expert on national television. When not in session or filming, Dr. Viviana enjoys spending quality time with her husband and their two children and going on adventures with family and friends. *The 4 Intimacy Styles* is her first book.

Find out more about Dr. Viviana Coles at:
www.DoctorViviana.com

Enjoyed this book so much you want to buy another for a friend?

Looking for Bulk Orders for your group or store?
Visit www.4IntimacyStyles.com for Sales Information

THE 4 INTIMACY STYLES